REDEFINING WEALTH MANAGEMENT

ACHIEVING WEALTH PRESERVATION WITH **HIGH RETURNS**

Turning Risk into Opportunity:
A Modern Framework for Wealth Managers

- 1st Edition -

Sidney Shauy, MBA

PALLAS VESTA
PUBLISHING CO. LLC

Published by Pallas Vesta Publishing Company LLC, New Jersey, USA

PALLAS VESTA
PUBLISHING CO. LLC

Pallas Vesta Publishing Company LLC
New Jersey, NJ – United States of America

Discounts for bulk sales are available. Please contact us by email below.

ISBN: 978-1-960691-12-5 (eBook)
ISBN: 978-1-960691-13-2 (Paperback)
First Edition: 2024

www.Engineering-Finance.com www.RISP500.com

Printed in the United States of America. Cover design by Microsoft CoPilot AI. Less than 25% of content assisted by ChatGPT.

SPECIAL THANKS

To my family, for their unconditional love and support, always

To my parents and grandparents, my eternal gratitude

To my mentors, for their wisdom and inspiration

GENERAL DISCLAIMER

While a great deal of care has been taken to provide accurate, informative, and helpful material on the subjects addressed in the book, neither the publisher nor the author is responsible for any errors and omissions, or the results obtained from the use of this information. The book contains ideas and opinions of the author. The strategies outlined in the book may not be suitable for every person under any circumstances, and they are not warranted or guaranteed to produce any particular results. The book is intended to provide general information for educational purposes only.

The book is sold with the understanding that neither the author nor the publisher is engaged in providing legal, business, financial, investment, tax, accounting, securities or any other professional advice. The author is not a licensed advisor. The reader should always consult with their own trusted and licensed professional advisors before adopting any of the suggested strategies in the book or drawing inferences from them. The contents of this book are provided "as is," without guarantees of accuracy, completeness, or timeliness regarding the results obtained from their use. The reader assumes full responsibility for the use of this information and uses it at their own risk. Neither the author nor the publisher will be liable for any direct, indirect, special, incidental, consequential, or punitive damages of any nature. In no event, whatsoever, will the author, Sidney Shauy, nor the publisher, Pallas Vesta Publishing Company LLC, their related companies, partners, agents, employees, associates, service providers, or their employees, be liable to readers or anyone for any decision or action taken in reliance on the contents of this book and its consequences. The information and all figures in this book that were accurate at the time of the writing may become inaccurate or outdated with the passage of time and by changes in the economy and markets. New laws and taxes may be enacted. Figures, including prices and rates, and assumptions are not guaranteed and are subject to change at any time. Any slights against individuals, groups, organizations, or companies are unintentional. Models used in the book are based on assumptions, which may or may not apply to everyone, and are subject to errors, omissions, and change. All models are simplifications of reality and must be understood as such. As in all models, assumptions, and numerical examples in the book, it has been stressed multiple times that individual results vary based on a wide range of factors related to each person's unique set of circumstances, needs, goals, quality of execution of strategies, in addition to uncontrollable factors, such as the moment and status of the economy and markets.

Clarification about references to S&P 500®:

S&P 500® is a trademark of S&P Global. It has nothing to do with the RISP 500™, which is a stock market risk metric developed by the authors based on data related to the S&P 500®, through a proprietary algorithm owned by Risk Scientific LLC.

About the Author

Sidney Shauy is an analytics-driven investor/trader using quantitative methods and risk management. The author has over 30 years of combined experience with world financial markets in leading global banks - Citigroup, Morgan Stanley, Lloyds Bank, ABN Amro, Bilbao Vizcaya, in New York, Hong Kong, and Sao Paulo - and real estate syndication investing and insurance structuring. In about 20 years, the author worked in all key functions in the trading floor: trading, portfolio management, structuring, and risk management. The author has managed multi-billion dollar portfolios for his employers successfully during multiple financial crises since the 1990s. In recent years, he worked with high net worth clients helping them strategize and structure investment portfolios and served as *subject matter expert* to prominent global strategy consulting firms on select projects. Expert in financial derivatives on multiple asset classes – stocks, currency, interest rates, commodities - including hybrid and exotic derivatives, he is constantly testing market data to develop new algorithms.

Automation engineer by training and quadrilingual, Sidney Shauy earned an MBA degree from the Wharton School at the University of Pennsylvania.

Site: www.Engineering-Finance.com

Blog: engineering-finance.medium.com

Site: www.risp500.com/

SIDNEY SHAUY

ENGINEERING FINANCE

Building Futures Together

Table of Contents

SYNOPSIS

REDEFINING WEALTH MANAGEMENT

The world of wealth management is familiar with this paradox: clients expect their wealth to be preserved and protected, even in volatile markets, yet they also want to see their assets outperform, no matter how challenging are the markets. But can you **deliver high returns without increasing risk?** If this challenge sounds familiar, you're not alone. We have all been there too. But what if there were a method to **consistently deliver both wealth protection AND high returns at the same time**? Here's what we found after years on the battlefield.

Note: ***Wealth Manager*** *in this book is referred to all investment professionals in general, including and not limited to Financial Advisors, RIAs, CFPs, Family Office Advisors, Wealth Managers, Portfolio Managers, Hedge Fund Managers, anyone with AUM responsibilities.*

ACHIEVING WEALTH PRESERVATION WITH **HIGH RETURNS**

1. Mission Impossible?

INTRODUCTION

Here's a scene too common in an advisor's office. A new HNW client walks in and declares right from the outset that their number 1 priority above all else is wealth preservation. But at the same time, they expect the advisor to deliver an outstanding performance. While the meaning of "outstanding performance" varies from client to client, even if it hasn't been verbalized word for word, you know deep down that clients always have great expectations from you. In general, "outstanding performance" may mean "beating a certain benchmark", or "achieving annual returns above a certain level (e.g., 10%)", or even simply "outperforming peer competitors in the industry". Nevertheless, whatever expectations your clients have from you, you know better than anyone that wealth preservation and high returns don't mix like oil and water. You've learned that they are antagonistic objectives: **earning a higher rate of return on an investment requires taking up higher risks**. For you, this is Economics 101, but clients still expect you to somehow perform an act of magic and make that happen. Sounds familiar?

The truth is that while no one can actually earn very high returns without increasing risks, it remains a non-issue. However, the moment the first wealth manager figures out how to crack the nut open, it will be a huge game changer for this professional. Clients will quickly line up to pour money in lifting this managers' AUM up to the stratosphere. It'd be every wealth manager's dream come true.

Maximizing the return-risk ratio is the way to achieve it but there has been a limit to the amount of optimization that can be accomplished, given the current state-of-the-art modern portfolio theory (MPT). The Efficient Frontier of a portfolio was one such attempt formulated by Harry Markowitz in 1952. Other best practices of MPT to optimize portfolio return-to-risk ratio include diversification and rebalancing/rotation of assets in portfolios from time to time.

But what else, besides the usual? Anything else that can impact portfolios in a more meaningful way?

THE INDUSTRY'S PERSISTENT PAIN POINT: OUTPERFORMANCE ISN'T CONSISTENT EVERY YEAR

Have you ever wondered why the goal of consistent outperformance eludes even the most seasoned wealth managers? The keyword here is consistency. Everyone in the wealth management industry has experienced periods of incredible outperformance at several moments in their careers. But even the most successful professionals have also experienced periods of lackluster results, including a few embarrassingly disastrous periods of losses caused by high volatility and uncertainty in the markets.

Why is so hard to maintain a high level of performance consistently, month after month, year after year?

We believe that **the answer lies not in a lack of skill but in a lack of the right tools**. Traditional wealth management techniques don't account for the complexity of today's market dynamics as we embark in a new era of increased volatility and uncertainty. Traditional risk management tools are also in a desperate need of a serious upgrade.

Meanwhile, clients don't care. They expect results. Or they will move their money elsewhere. Many are even embracing DIY passive index investing. They don't see the struggle financial professionals face every day behind the scenes to deliver them the best results possible.

DIAGNOSING UNDERPERFORMANCE

We have all been there. Who hasn't experienced periods of underperformance? Even the most successful investors in the world did. There are just so many factors at play that may lead to underperformance, but still, we need to map them out, so we can learn how to make the right changes in our practice to avoid them. I'm going to list the 10 top culprits for underperformance and later offer a solution to mitigate their damaging effects - all at once with a single solution:

1. Taking too much risk for the return earned (risk is often not properly quantified)
2. Losses due to a sudden market correction or crash (unexpected turn of events)

3. Difficulty making right decisions in key moments (volatility and ambiguity in the markets)
4. Wrong, partial, or conflicting information (also false beliefs) leading to bad decisions
5. Psychological biases and false memories clouding judgment leading to bad decisions
6. Excessive, insufficient, or poor portfolio diversification (sub-optimal return-to-risk ratio)
7. Stock prices not behaving logically based on fundamentals (e.g., market rallying on poor fundamentals or vice-versa) happening too often
8. Conflicting expert opinions with equally compelling arguments leading to confusion resulting in wrong decisions too often (bulls vs. bears)
9. Acting too late to follow trends or too early on contrarian views (poor market timing)
10. The S&P 500® benchmark is just too hard to beat

I'm pretty sure this list didn't come as a surprise to you. One way or another, you must already be familiar with these issues, because they affect every one of us in the industry. The point now is whether you have a good solution to resolve them properly, creating the conditions for consistent outperformance to take root.

Issue #1 is the most often overlooked and the #1 reason for portfolios to bleed money or perform below potential. This happens because returns are just not high enough to compensate for the risk taken. You must always ask yourself if the risks you are currently exposing your portfolios to are being properly rewarded by the actual returns you are earning. It turns out that the majority of investors and investment professionals aren't quantifying their risks properly, if at all, before making investment decisions. Unfortunately, risk is seldom given the same level of scrutiny as potential returns. In macro, fundamental, and technical analysis, the focus is always placed on potential returns and much less attention is given to risk, isn't it? It's not anyone's fault: there simply aren't appropriate tools around for the job.

Risk is a matter of probabilities. How often probabilities and win-loss odds are quantified and scrutinized before investment decisions are made? As a result, more often than not, investors and wealth managers aren't fully aware of the actual risks their portfolios are exposed to, let alone knowing whether their actual returns are compensating well for the risks taken. (note: VAR measures risk but it's a reactive tool to reduce risk; it's not a tool to make investment decisions). Then, all it takes to underperform is just a slight increase in the market risk for even the best laid out plans to go out of the window. The first step to resolve this blind spot's vulnerability is to start quantifying risks properly and optimize return-to-risk ratios. In this book, you will learn how.

The solution we are going to present in this book will solve all the above issues once and for all. Always remember that we are only entitled for the privilege of earning a ROI because we took risks for it. **The more we can learn from this relationship by quantifying risks and adjusting portfolios accordingly to maximize return-to-risk ratios, the better conditions we create for a sustained long-term outperformance**.

THE CHALLENGE IS ONLY GETTING BIGGER FOR WEALTH MANAGERS

The U.S. stock market has enjoyed an impressive 80-year run, fueling the myth that "*stocks always go up in the long run*." Post-WWII, the U.S. dollar's status as the world reserve currency helped create the largest and most powerful stock market in the history of humanity. However, the future for the conditions that supported this impressive growth is highly uncertain.

Tectonic shifts occurring once in a century are gradually and silently altering the global economic order. The BRICS countries are overtaking the G7, and the U.S. faces increasing competition from China in key technologies of the future. De-globalization and rising protectionism are taking shape. Domestically, income and wealth inequalities are impacting GDP growth, twin deficits keep ballooning, and we saw the end of the 30-year low inflation and the 40-year bond bull market. Even the total dominance of the U.S. dollar is for the first time ever being challenged.

Market volatility has increased since 2018, with lower returns forecasted for the S&P 500® over the next decade by Goldman Sachs and JP Morgan. Volatility for stocks and bonds is expected to rise further. Lower returns with higher risks are exactly the worst combination that can happen!

Besides, we are seeing the explosive growth of index funds, outpacing actively managed funds, and now even HNW clients allocate at least some portion of their portfolios to passive investing. On the financial professional's business side, AI-driven disruptions (e.g., AI-powered advisors, etc.) are likely to challenge business models in the wealth management industry itself.

Wealth managers must quickly adapt to all these changes to succeed. Embracing innovation with an open mind, new technology, better data analytics, and new tools for fast and accurate decision-making will be essential to survive and thrive in this fast evolving and challenging landscape.

MISSION IMPOSSIBLE?

For decades, the financial industry has wrestled with a problem so daunting that many have resigned themselves to believe it's unsolvable: **achieving wealth preservation while simultaneously earning really high returns**. The prevailing wisdom says you must take on greater risks to unlock greater returns—a notion we don't dispute. Risk and return are inherently linked, and eliminating risk entirely would leave you with minuscule returns, like the meager yields of U.S. Treasury bills. But what if we reframed the challenge? What if, instead of merely accepting risk as a necessary evil, we optimized its role in the equation? The goal isn't to reduce risk to zero—that would be counterproductive. Instead, **the mission is to maximize the return-to-risk ratio, extracting the highest potential return for every unit of risk accepted**. While wealth managers and industry researchers have proposed various intriguing strategies to approach this balance, we dared to take an innovative step forward: achieving this elusive goal by turning the tables on risk itself.

We dared to prove it isn't mission impossible. We will show you in the book how we were able to achieve **much higher return-to-risk ratios** than holding the S&P 500® index itself!

For now, just take a peek at the results of 8 strategies implemented since 1/1/2022:

2022 to Date Performance Ranking 1-Jul-2024

Asset/Strategy	Cum. Return	CAGR	Max DD	RoMaD
Strategy 8	**210.17%**	56.26%	**-14.88%**	**14.1x**
Strategy 7	**209.75%**	56.17%	**-22.78%**	**9.2x**
Strategy 5	**207.66%**	55.76%	**-21.16%**	**9.8x**
Strategy 4	**183.33%**	50.78%	**-31.70%**	**5.8x**
Strategy 6	**177.22%**	49.49%	**-15.75%**	**11.3x**
Strategy 3	**121.19%**	36.76%	**-18.58%**	**6.5x**
Strategy 2	**77.84%**	25.48%	**-14.52%**	**5.4x**
Strategy 1	**55.81%**	19.11%	**-8.72%**	**6.4x**
SPY (S&P 500)	**14.82%**	**5.60%**	**-25.51%**	**0.6x**

Max DD: Maximum Drawdowns, RoMaD: Return over Maximum Drawdowns
Since 01 Jan 2022. Cumulative return is compounded daily.

First, note how in 2 ½ years, **ALL 8 STRATEGIES ARE SERIOUSLY OUTPERFORMING THE S&P 500®**. We will detail each of the strategies shortly. They are ordered by increasing risk; i.e., Strategy 1 is the most conservative and Strategy 8 is the most aggressive. We wanted to cover a wide spectrum of risk tolerance possibilities. Note also that:

- The period included a bear market (2022) and a bull market (2023-2024), coupled with many volatile periods.
- Even riskier strategies than simply holding the S&P 500® (SPY) experienced **lower** maximum drawdowns, while delivering **much higher** returns.
- **All strategies have delivered substantially higher RoMaD (Return over Maximum Drawdown, a key return-to-risk ratio) than the S&P 500® itself. This is how we are achieving wealth protection with high returns!**

How did we do this? Keep reading and you will soon find out!

A SURPRISINGLY SIMPLE SOLUTION?

It's hard to believe that something so effective can be so simple to use, yet that's exactly the case with the RISP 500™ solution based on the SMIGRM framework ("Stock Market Investing Guided by Risk Management"). While the algorithm powering this breakthrough solution is rooted in a decade of rigorous research, testing, and refinement, the user experience is refreshingly straightforward. You don't need a PhD in finance, advanced programming skills, or hours of technical analysis to harness its power. All you need is less than 5 minutes a day to read the daily RISP 500™ risk indicator, select the maximum risk cutoff level (RPT, to be explained later in the book) based on the investor's personal risk tolerance/appetite, and let the RISP 500™ guide you toward smarter investment decisions. For the user, it's really easy as 1-2-3.

The RISP 500™ ("Risk Index for the S&P 500") quantifies the risk embedded in the stock market at any given moment in time. Its daily once a day measurement, taken between 10 a.m. and noon ET, is perfect for long-term investors and wealth managers focused on helping their clients achieve steady growth and preservation of wealth over time. For those battling the market's twists and turns—such as day traders looking to capitalize on short-term opportunities or hedge fund managers striving to eke out every possible basis point of return—the All Day Long Real-Time RISP 500™ indicator provides continuous updates, offering an edge in highly dynamic environments.

That's it. There's no complex setup, no intricate strategies to learn, and no need to spend hours poring over charts. Whether you're a wealth manager overseeing millions in assets or an everyday investor focused on protecting and growing your retirement savings, using the RISP 500™ system is not only possible—it's surprisingly easy.

WHAT RISP 500™ CAN DO FOR YOUR STOCK PORTFOLIOS

The RISP 500™ isn't just an indicator; it offers a powerful 3-in-1 benefit framework that addresses your most pressing challenges while unlocking untapped opportunities for growth and risk management. In simple terms, here's the top 3 things the RISP 500™ can do for you:

1. Wealth Protection First: Early Crash Detection

Your hard-earned wealth deserves to be shielded from devastating market crashes. The RISP 500™ acts as an early warning system, alerting you to elevated risk levels before trouble strikes. The best way to avoid the pain of digging out of a deep financial hole (and time wasted) is by not falling into one in the first place. With the RISP 500™ guiding your moves, you can proactively protect your portfolio from sudden drawdowns, ensuring wealth preservation remains always your top priority.

2. Market Timing Advantage

Timing the market isn't impossible—it just requires the right tools. The RISP 500™ gives you the ability to not only avoid downturns but also capitalize on higher return opportunities when risks are favorable. As a result, this indicator allows you to enhance your net performance by aligning your moves with the market's rhythm. It even integrates seamlessly into your existing portfolio management practice, boosting your overall strategy with precision timing.

3. Explore Risk for Maximum Return

Achieving superior returns isn't about eliminating risk but about managing it effectively. The RISP 500™ enables you to maximize your portfolio's return-to-risk ratio (Sharpe, RoMaD, etc.) by letting you differentiate which risks are worth taking and which are not, given the client's own risk tolerance/appetite. To outperform, we must make sure we are always properly rewarded for the amount of risk we are taking. This is accomplished by tactically allocating assets to match prevailing risk environments (a concept called **Context-Dependent Dynamic Asset Allocation** – soon to be properly introduced later in the book), turning risk into a strategic advantage.

By combining these benefits, the RISP 500™ transforms how you approach wealth management, ensuring that you not only preserve what you've built but also grow it with confidence.

INTEGRATING RISP 500™ SEAMLESSLY INTO YOUR PRACTICE

As a wealth manager, you've honed your expertise and built a strong foundation of skills to serve your clients effectively. The introduction of the RISP 500™ solution doesn't require you to overhaul your approach or make drastic changes to your routine. It's not here to replace your trusted methods or disrupt your day-to-day activities or change what you do best. Instead, the RISP 500™ is designed to complement and enhance what you already do, seamlessly integrating into your existing strategies and amplifying your ability to deliver exceptional results.

This innovative tool provides critical daily insights into market risk levels, empowering you to make better, more informed decisions for your clients. Whether you use the RISP 500™ as an additional layer of guidance or as a key driver for tactical adjustments, it works in harmony with your existing portfolio management processes.

The best part? Adding this powerful tool to your arsenal requires virtually no effort. Subscribing to the daily RISP 500™ indicator is simple, and for a **limited time, it's entirely FREE. Yes, FREE!** There's **absolutely no cost or risk to give it a try**. If you're not completely satisfied, you can cancel at any time with no obligations or hidden fees. What do you have to lose? This is a no-brainer **opportunity to explore the RISP 500™'s potential and see firsthand how it can transform your practice, helping you achieve stronger, more consistent long-term outperformance for your clients while setting yourself apart in the industry and grow your AUM**.

In the coming brave new world of heightened market volatility and uncertain returns, staying ahead requires the right tools. The RISP 500™ offers precisely that—an essential solution to help you navigate the complexities of modern wealth management with confidence and precision. Why wait? **SIGN UP NOW WHILE IT'S FREE** and see how this no-risk offer can unlock unparalleled opportunities for your practice and your clients.

2. Turning the Table on Risk

A VISION BORN FROM CRISIS

You may be wondering how we came up with this new framework solution that resulted in the performance we presented you earlier. It actually started about 15 years ago! In the aftermath of the 2008 Great Financial Crisis, few financial professionals could confidently claim they saw it coming. The crash decimated markets and wiped out countless portfolios, and it raised an unsettling question: how could such massive risk go unnoticed by so many seasoned experts?

After all, looking back it is clear that the 2008 GFC didn't happen overnight. The descent from the top took several months to reach the bottom. So why did so many people lose so much money?

For those in wealth management, responsible for clients' wealth, the stakes were particularly high. **The primary goal was—and remains—the protection and growth of client wealth, but 2008 proved how vulnerable even the most diversified portfolios could be to systemic risk.**

For me, that crisis marked a turning point. My mission became clear: to develop a reliable, proactive system to anticipate market downturns before they happen. But that was easier said than done. Early attempts at developing an algorithm failed; the techniques and data we had simply weren't enough to provide the predictive power needed. However, **the seed had been planted**. It was only after almost 10 long years, while I obsessively continued to test, research, and refine models that a framework of what we believed might ultimately transform wealth management by redefining how we understand and manage risk, was gradually emerging.

MY PATH TO SMIGRM: STOCK MARKET INVESTING GUIDED BY RISK MANAGEMENT

After the 2008 GFC, a group of traders and quants, including myself, began brainstorming ways to prevent another financial disaster. At the time, I was trading interest rate derivatives for an international bank in New York while attending courses at a master's degree in Mathematics in Finance at NYU Courant Institute. With 15 years of experience in trading and risk management back then, I started developing models to detect minute data changes to provide early market crash warnings. Despite numerous attempts and collaborations, none of the models met the standards for an effective early warning system, and our research lab was eventually shut down.

However, I never gave up. Traditional tools like technical, fundamental, and macro analysis often failed to provide actionable answers early and during market turmoil—the times when reliable tools were most needed. This glaring gap fueled my determination to find a solution.

In fact, I am no stranger to a financial crisis. I grew up in Brazil when hyperinflation reached 3% a day! My banking career started with the Mexican Crisis in the early 1990s, followed by the Asian Crisis, the Russian Crisis, and the Max-devaluation of the Brazilian Real. Having experienced multiple crises firsthand while managing billion-dollar portfolios for my employers, plus later crashes like the 2000 dot-com bubble, 2008 GFC, and 2020 Covid Crash, I learned countless lessons (the hard way) and knew that far stronger risk management tools were desperately needed. After years of research and failure, the breakthrough came with emerging insights into new VIX products, new research, and better data. I also learned from the work of some very smart people. Leveraging this knowledge, I built and refined new models incorporating data from multiple markets and macroeconomic variables. Still, it took over a decade of trials and errors to refine the algorithm that could ultimately deliver consistent, robust results in live trading.

Our efforts led to the creation of SMIGRM—Stock Market Investing *Guided by* Risk Management—a customizable framework designed to help investors optimize their return-risk balance. On

January 3, 2022, we launched live trading of 8 strategies using our best prototype algorithm, which produced the RISP 500™, a proprietary risk indicator for the S&P 500®. More than an early crash detector, our goal evolved to the creation of a framework or tool that investors could easily customize to fit their own risk-return profiles to achieve their objectives. This innovation now serves as a powerful tool for wealth preservation and benchmark-beating returns.

A more complete formulation of SMIGRM with technical details is laid out in my previous book titled **Stock Market Investing Guided by Risk Management** (235 pages on paperback or 231 pages hardcover) – available on Amazon.com.

IS YOUR CURRENT ASSET ALLOCATION ROADBLOCKING YOUR OUTPERFORMANCE?

Asset allocation is the go-to strategy for weathering market downturns, with the 60/40 stock-to-bond portfolio being the most popular choice. This approach assumes a low or negative correlation between stocks and bonds, but history tells a different story. In 2002, for example, both the S&P 500® and bonds posted significant losses, showing that this correlation can break under certain conditions influenced by inflation, interest rates, and economic growth.

Even if bonds consistently hedged stock losses, the trade-off is clear: sacrificing returns for safety. Vanguard's 60/40 fund (VBIAX), for instance, has delivered a 6.70% annualized return since 2000—lower than a 100% stock portfolio due to permanent return dampening. Similarly, "All Weather" portfolios popularized by Ray Dalio face the same limitation: while static allocations permanently hedge for all conditions, it sacrifice gains in favorable markets.

So, why not allocate 100% to stocks during favorable conditions and rotate to safer assets in turbulent times? This is the core idea behind SMIGRM's **Context-Dependent Dynamic Asset Allocation**—a strategy designed to optimize overall returns by aligning assets with the prevailing risk environment, transforming static portfolios into dynamic ones that perform optimally in all scenarios.

SMIGRM IN ACTION:
CONTEXT-DEPENDENT DYNAMIC ASSET ALLOCATION

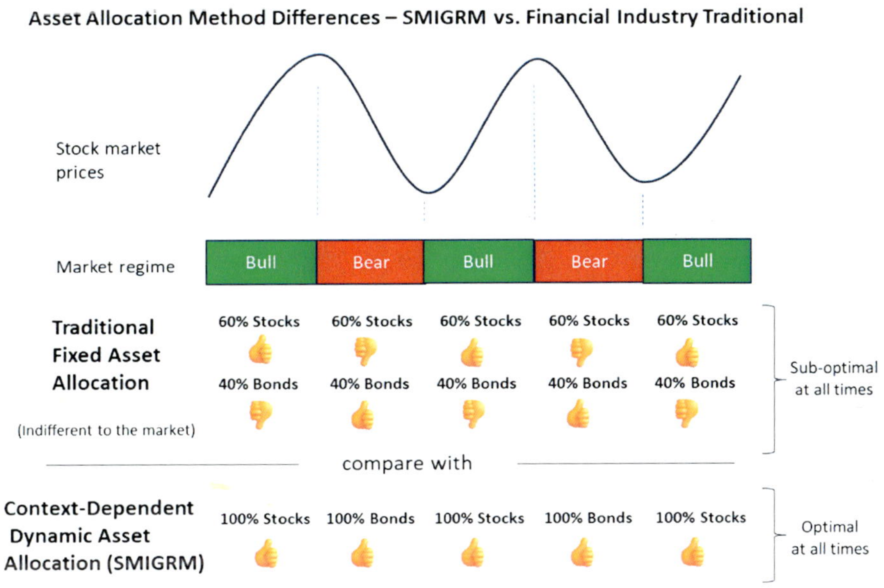

SMIGRM redefines portfolio management with **Context-Dependent Dynamic Asset Allocation**, where decisions are driven by real-time risk assessments via the **RISP 500**™ indicator. Unlike static models like 60/40 or "All Weather" portfolios, this approach dynamically adjusts asset allocation based on market risk levels:

- **Low Risk:** The RISP 500™ signals allocation to high-return assets like equity ETFs (e.g., SPY or QQQ).

- **High Risk:** The indicator prompts a shift to safe assets such as gold, bonds, or cash, prioritizing wealth preservation over returns.

This dynamic reallocation ensures portfolios remain optimized for all prevailing conditions, unlike static allocations that perform sub-optimally across scenarios. For instance, a simple two-risk level strategy might allocate between SPY and cash, dynamically adapting to the market's risk environment.

Here's an example of a two-risk level setup of a simple strategy with a risk asset and a safe asset:

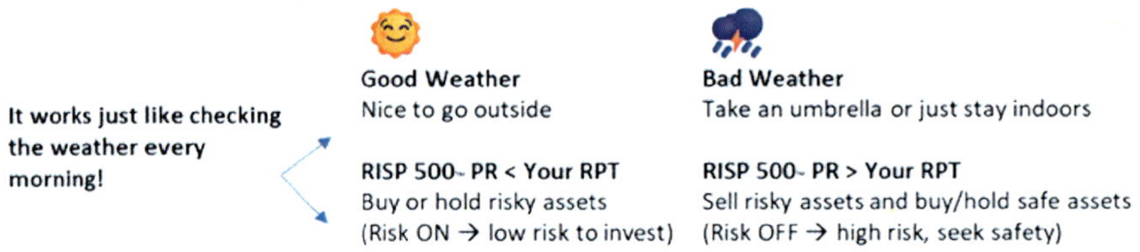

Why Risk-Dependent Asset Allocation Works

SMIGRM's approach is rooted in three principles:

1. **Risk Aversion Principle:** Rising risk leads investors to seek safety, pushing risky asset prices down and vice-versa—a causal relationship, which is much stronger than just correlation.
2. **Risk-Reward Dynamics:** Returns are compensation for risk taken. No risk, no reward; higher risk increases the probability of higher returns.
3. **Risk as proxy for Win-Loss Odds:** Traditional measures like volatility treat gains and losses equally, while SMIGRM uses the RISP 500™ to quantify risk as a proxy for probabilities of market direction. Higher RISP 500™ values indicate statistically unfavorable odds for holding risky assets and vice-versa.

Unlike traditional tools that react to risk (e.g., Value-at-Risk), SMIGRM leverages risk proactively, guiding decisions to seek safety early and optimize portfolio performance at all times.

2022 to Date Performance Ranking 1-Jul-2024

Asset/Strategy	Cum. Return	CAGR	Max DD	RoMaD
Strategy 8	**210.17%**	56.26%	**-14.88%**	**14.1x**
Strategy 7	**209.75%**	56.17%	**-22.78%**	**9.2x**
Strategy 5	**207.66%**	55.76%	**-21.16%**	**9.8x**
Strategy 4	**183.33%**	50.78%	**-31.70%**	**5.8x**
Strategy 6	**177.22%**	49.49%	**-15.75%**	**11.3x**
Strategy 3	**121.19%**	36.76%	**-18.58%**	**6.5x**
Strategy 2	**77.84%**	25.48%	**-14.52%**	**5.4x**
Strategy 1	**55.81%**	19.11%	**-8.72%**	**6.4x**
SPY (S&P 500)	**14.82%**	**5.60%**	**-25.51%**	**0.6x**

Max DD: Maximum Drawdowns, RoMaD: Return over Maximum Drawdowns
Since 01 Jan 2022. Cumulative return is compounded daily.

A more complete formulation of SMIGRM with technical details is laid out in my previous book titled **Stock Market Investing Guided by Risk Management** (235 pages on paperback or 231 pages hardcover) – available on Amazon.com.

3. The Secret to Investment Success in a Probabilistic World

Human evolution has conditioned us to seek certainty and avoid randomness. We like things that are deterministic: it gives us a sense of security and inner peace. After all, the ability to make cause-effect associations quickly enabled the survival of our species. We prefer deterministic formulas like Newton's law of gravity, which provide precise outcomes. However, like most things in life, the investment world operates in a highly probabilistic environment, where outcomes are uncertain and risk is ever-present. Unfortunately, the investment management industry (and many in academia as well) treat investing as if it were deterministic (or assume a high degree of determinism), by focusing on macro views, fundamentals, and forecasts while neglecting the critical tools of probabilities and statistics. This oversight ultimately leads to insufficient returns earned for the amount of risk taken. In other words, sub-optimal return-to-risk ratios for investments is widespread throughout the industry.

The key to long-term investing success lies in understanding and leveraging the probabilistic nature of markets. SMIGRM introduces a groundbreaking formula that combines three essential pillars for success in a probabilistic world: Statistical Edge, Asymmetrical Payoff, and the Law of Large Numbers. Together, these elements create a framework that maximizes returns while managing risks effectively.

THE FORMULA TO SUCCESS:
STATISTICAL EDGE + ASYMMETRICAL PAYOFF + LAW OF LARGE NUMBERS

1. Statistical Edge

In investing, no outcome is guaranteed, but decisions should be guided by probabilities. A **Statistical Edge** ensures that investments are made when the odds favor success. SMIGRM uses the RISP 500™ risk indicator to identify low-risk, high-return opportunities, signaling when to enter or exit markets based on real-time risk data, based on the investor's own risk tolerance/appetite. This approach mirrors a poker player's strategy—playing only when the odds are favorable.

2. Asymmetrical Payoff

An **Asymmetrical Payoff** means ensuring potential rewards far outweigh the risks. SMIGRM is designed to limit losses early while allowing unlimited upside potential run its course. Investors often fall into the trap of holding losing stocks too long and selling winning stocks too soon, but SMIGRM enforces discipline by design, flipping the odds in favor of positive payoffs.

3. Law of Large Numbers

Success in the probabilistic world relies on consistency over time. The **Law of Large Numbers** ensures that investments made with a favorable Statistical Edge and a positive Asymmetrical Payoff strategically built in, with enough repetitions over time, outcomes align with favorable probabilities towards success. Just as casinos assure profitability through small statistical edges repeated over thousands of games, investors using SMIGRM are strategically positioned to accumulate profits by consistently applying the strategy over time.

By combining these three elements—favoring probabilities, positively biased payoffs, and repeating the process over time—investors create a strategy akin to a casino's, where discipline and statistical advantage will pay off leading to consistent success over time.

THE SMIGRM ADVANTAGE: ALWAYS INVESTING WITH FAVORABLE ODDS

Stock prices don't follow predictable patterns; they move probabilistically. The key to success isn't predicting every move but executing a strategically favorable system with discipline, investing only when the odds favor a positive outcome. Imagine being fully invested in high-growth assets during favorable markets and shifting to safety before downturns. Over time, this **"risk-on, risk-off"** strategy builds cumulative returns, safeguarding client portfolios and outperforming benchmarks like the S&P 500®. It will give you the best chances to beat the S&P 500® because a buy & hold of the index (or passively investing in index funds) is a permanent "risk-on" of the index. SMIGRM will enable passive investors to add periods of "risk-off" when the RISP 500™ indicator reveals risk building up in the market above their own tolerance levels for risk.

Ironically, stock buy & holders and passive index investors think they are playing the safe game, where in fact, they are exposed to the market's systematic risk 100% of the time! As a result, their return-to-risk ratio will be sub-optimal. For example, the maximum drawdown experienced by the SPY (S&P 500® ETF) since 2022 (last 2.5 years) was -25.51%. In the same period, the SPY returned +14.82% (from 1/1/2022 to 7/1/2024). Our 8 strategies based on SMIGRM (see tables below) delivered much higher RoMaDs in the same period (5.4x to 14.1x) than SPY (0.6x)!

Ranked by Cumulative Return

2022 to Date Performance Ranking 1-Jul-2024

Asset/Strategy	Cum. Return	CAGR	Max DD	RoMaD
Strategy 8	**210.17%**	56.26%	**-14.88%**	**14.1x**
Strategy 7	**209.75%**	56.17%	**-22.78%**	**9.2x**
Strategy 5	**207.66%**	55.76%	**-21.16%**	**9.8x**
Strategy 4	**183.33%**	50.78%	**-31.70%**	**5.8x**
Strategy 6	**177.22%**	49.49%	**-15.75%**	**11.3x**
Strategy 3	**121.19%**	36.76%	**-18.58%**	**6.5x**
Strategy 2	**77.84%**	25.48%	**-14.52%**	**5.4x**
Strategy 1	**55.81%**	19.11%	**-8.72%**	**6.4x**
SPY (S&P 500)	**14.82%**	**5.60%**	**-25.51%**	**0.6x**

Max DD: Maximum Drawdowns, RoMaD: Return over Maximum Drawdowns
Since 01 Jan 2022. Cumulative return is compounded daily.

Ranked by RoMaD

2022 to Date Performance Ranking 1-Jul-2024

Asset/Strategy	Cum. Return	CAGR	Max DD	RoMaD
Strategy 8	**210.17%**	56.26%	**-14.88%**	**14.1x**
Strategy 6	**177.22%**	49.49%	**-15.75%**	**11.3x**
Strategy 5	**207.66%**	55.76%	**-21.16%**	**9.8x**
Strategy 7	**209.75%**	56.17%	**-22.78%**	**9.2x**
Strategy 3	**121.19%**	36.76%	**-18.58%**	**6.5x**
Strategy 1	**55.81%**	19.11%	**-8.72%**	**6.4x**
Strategy 4	**183.33%**	50.78%	**-31.70%**	**5.8x**
Strategy 2	**77.84%**	25.48%	**-14.52%**	**5.4x**
SPY (S&P 500)	**14.82%**	**5.60%**	**-25.51%**	**0.6x**

Max DD: Maximum Drawdowns, RoMaD: Return over Maximum Drawdowns
Since 01 Jan 2022. Cumulative return is compounded daily.

Think about it. Stock diversification helped you mitigate non-systematic risk. But you are still left with systematic risk. What to do about it? Traditionally, you would use a static allocation with bonds or other low correlation assets.

Ok, but **where are you going to find low or negative correlation assets if almost all asset classes have <u>positive correlation with</u>**

stocks? Correlations with stocks vary over time, but the lowest are bonds (-0.08) and gold (+0.08). How good is that? Remember the tragedy that was year 2022... In addition, sudden and unexpected shifts in correlation can destroy portfolios: it's itself a risk! **SMIGRM offers a more efficient solution that does even NOT require correlation to work!**

At its core, SMIGRM works on a different set of principles and is about **turning the tables on risk**. It's no wonder it's delivering much stronger results and with consistency. Embrace a better paradigm that views risk as a strategic tool for maximizing returns while preserving wealth.

SMIGRM isn't just a new method; it's a new standard in wealth management—one that optimizes your return for every bit of risk taken. **With SMIGRM, you don't just take any risk but only those risks worth taking**. Are you ready to turn risk into your greatest asset?

Roger Federer, during the commencement speech to the Dartmouth College Class of 2024 revealed that despite winning almost 80% of all singles tennis matches in his entire career, on a point-by-point basis, his point-win rate was only 54%.

It's almost a 1:1 win-loss ratio but Roger's ***small edge of 4%*** *was all he needed to become one of the greatest of all time.*

---

4. Market Timing Finally Becomes Possible

For years, market timing has been dismissed as an unachievable goal. The belief was simple: predicting market highs and lows was too unreliable, often leading to poor results. Everyone who attempted failed. However, it doesn't prove market timing is impossible. We dared to disagree: **SMIGRM's Context-Dependent Dynamic Asset Allocation, powered by the RISP 500™ index**, has challenged this notion. By basing allocation decisions on real-time risk data instead of speculative predictions, SMIGRM has been proven to make market timing a practical and reliable tool.

Unlike traditional methods relying on forecasting or historical chart patterns, SMIGRM aligns asset allocation with the current risk environment. The RISP 500™ analyzes market volatility, economic indicators, and other variables to generate an objective risk score, guiding timely asset rotation. This approach avoids the pitfalls of guesswork, enabling wealth managers to naturally "buy low and sell high" by adapting to real-time market conditions. The result is enhanced performance and significantly reduced exposure during downturns.

With live trading results proving its effectiveness, SMIGRM demonstrates that market timing based on data-driven insights is not only possible but also a game-changing advantage in wealth management.

LOW TURNOVER:
A GREAT ADDED BENEFIT OF SMIGRM

Dynamic asset allocation may raise concerns about frequent trading, which can erode returns through transaction costs and taxes. However, SMIGRM's Context-Dependent Dynamic Asset Allocation maintains **impressively low turnover—typically averaging one trade every two weeks or less**. Turnover may increase in volatile markets with more frequent rotations as SMIGRM works hard to protect wealth, but in normal, stable markets, this frequency drops further as assets remain aligned with favorable conditions.

Unlike traditional rebalancing, which adjusts portfolios at fixed intervals, SMIGRM responds dynamically to meaningful changes in market risk, ensuring efficiency and precision.

This low-turnover approach minimizes friction costs while optimizing portfolios for the current risk environment. For wealth managers, it offers a sustainable and cost-effective way to manage client portfolios, delivering consistent performance while maintaining efficiency. SMIGRM combines strategic adaptability with practicality, making it an invaluable tool for modern wealth management.

CONCLUSION: REDEFINING WEALTH MANAGEMENT

Context-Dependent Dynamic Asset Allocation represents a significant advancement in wealth management, shifting away from static, one-size-fits-all models to an adaptive, context-driven approach that aligns asset allocation with real-time market conditions. This method empowers wealth managers to break free from the extreme dependency on correlation (to stay low and stable) and the limitations of traditional asset allocation frameworks, which often sacrifice performance for safety by holding fixed asset mixes across all market environments.

Through its data-driven risk assessment, this approach **redefines Market Timing as a viable strategy** for capturing upside and avoiding downturns. By rotating assets based on the RISP 500™'s real-time risk measurement, **wealth managers can protect client portfolios during turbulent times and capitalize on growth during stable periods**. Additionally, the model's low turnover rate ensures that changes are meaningful, minimizing unnecessary trades and related costs.

SMIGRM isn't just a new strategy—it's a new way of understanding and managing risk in wealth management. By turning risk into an advantage, it gives wealth managers the tools to deliver results that can exceed client expectations and build lasting trust. Are you ready to embrace a modern, easy to execute, data-driven approach to wealth management?

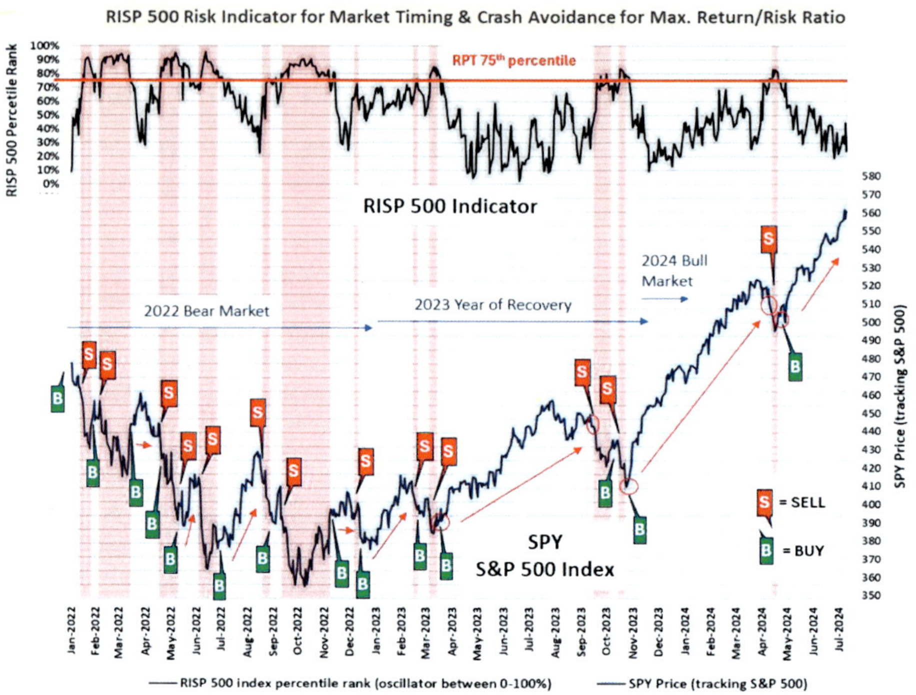
RISP 500 Risk Indicator for Market Timing & Crash Avoidance for Max. Return/Risk Ratio
RISP 500 Percetile Rank
RPT 75th percentile
RISP 500 Indicator
2022 Bear Market
2023 Year of Recovery
2024 Bull Market
SPY
S&P 500 Index
S = SELL
B = BUY
SPY Price (tracking S&P 500)
RISP 500 index percentile rank (oscillator between 0-100%)
SPY Price (tracking S&P 500)

5. How to Use the RISP 500 Indicator for Wealth Management

The **RISP 500™** is a cutting-edge risk measurement tool designed to help investors make data-driven decisions in the stock market. By analyzing over 15 critical variables across markets—such as bonds, currencies, and equities—the RISP 500™ consolidates this information into a single risk score that reflects the current risk environment. This algorithm is dynamic—it's constantly put to the test and recalibrated to adapt to fundamental market changes, by adding or removing variables as necessary to stay accurate over time. This adaptability ensures that the indicator remains accurate, accounting for interconnected factors like interest rates and volatility fluctuations that influence stock prices and investor sentiment.

The key feature is the **RISP 500™ Percentile Rank**, which compares current risk levels to historical data since 2008. For example, a score in the 80th percentile indicates that today's risk level is higher than 80% of all past values measured in the last 15 years. This historical context empowers investors to gauge the intensity of market risk currently measured and make informed choices about whether to stay invested in risk assets or shift to safer assets.

For the RISP 500™ risk indicator, we don't use its absolute value but the <u>**RISP 500™ Percentile Rank**</u>.

PERSONALIZING YOUR RISK PERCENTILE THRESHOLD (RPT)

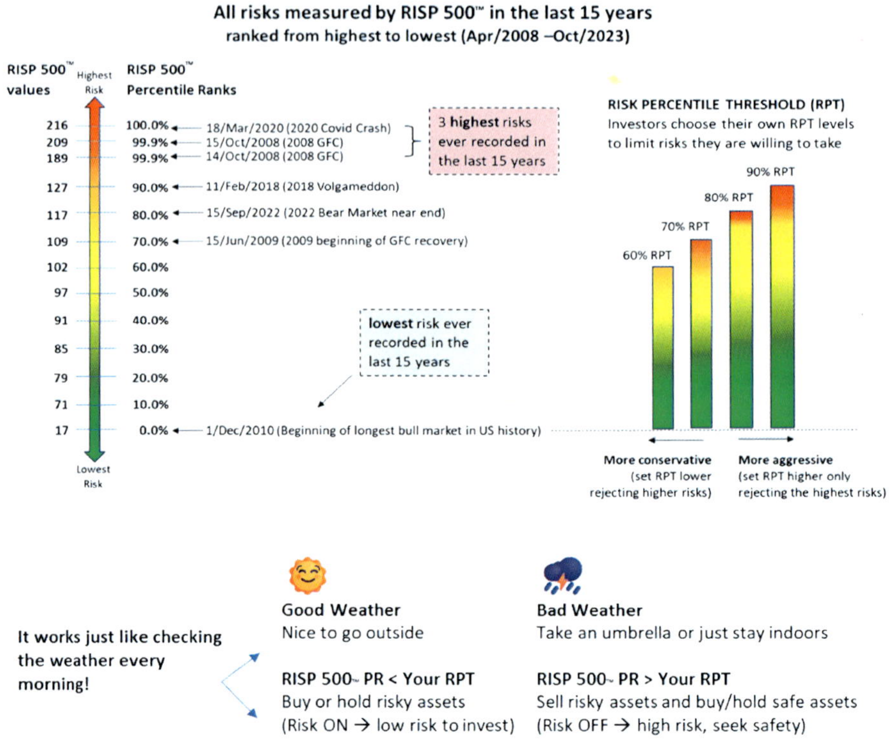

The **Risk Percentile Threshold (RPT)** allows investors to customize their approach to risk management. The RPT serves as the cutoff level for switching between "Risk ON" (holding riskier assets) and "Risk OFF" (rotating to safer assets).

- **Conservative investors** may want to choose a lower RPT, such as 65% or 70%, exiting the market earlier when risks rise.
- **Moderate investors** may want to pick an intermediate RPT, such as 75% or 80%.

- **Aggressive investors** might opt for a higher RPT, like 85%, 90%, or even 95%, maintaining exposure longer to capture higher returns.

This flexibility lets investors tailor their strategies to align with their risk tolerance and investment goals. Investors can adjust their RPT over time, raising it if they seek more exposure or lowering it if they want to reduce risk. A simple two-level risk system enables investors to toggle between holding riskier assets (like an index ETF) when risk is low and rotating to safer options (like cash) when risk is high. More sophisticated setups allow for three or more risk levels, offering additional flexibility and granularity to choose assets that best align with each risk level.

By combining the RISP 500™ with an RPT, investors have a powerful tool for risk-based decision-making, providing clarity and control over market exposure in both stable and volatile periods.

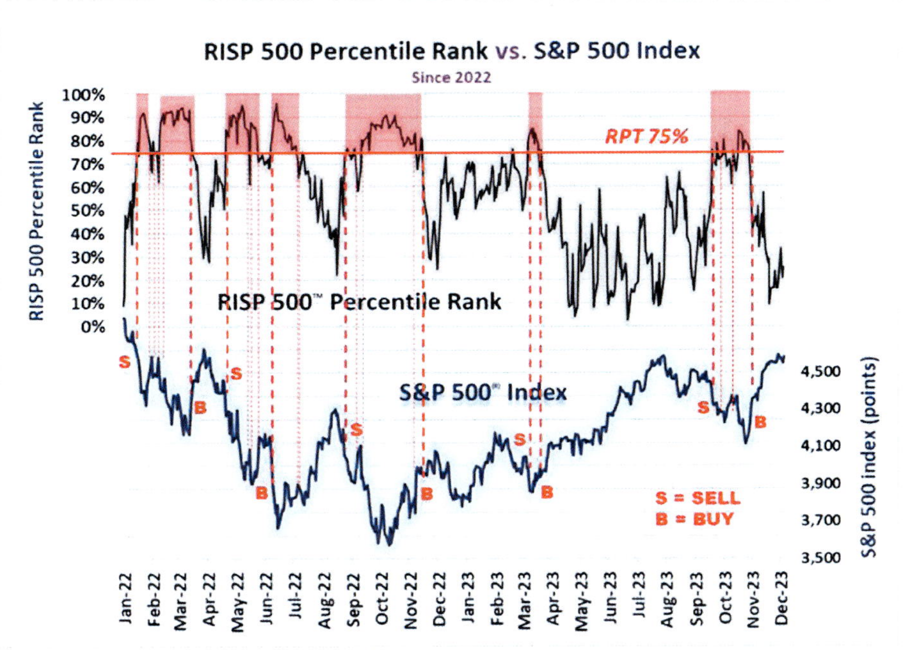

UNDERSTANDING HOW RPT AFFECT YOUR RESULTS

Your chosen RPT directly influences your investment results. For example:

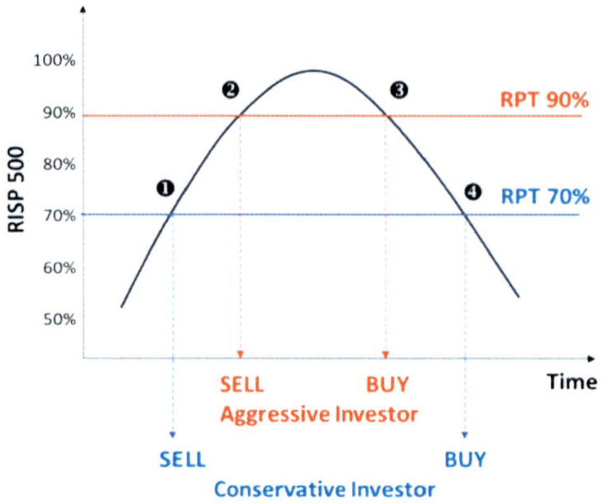

- A Conservative Investor with an RPT of 70% exits the market sooner, reducing exposure when risks rises.
- An Aggressive Investor with an RPT of 90% stays in the market longer, benefiting from potential gains during elevated risk periods.
- When risks decrease, the Aggressive Investor re-enters the market earlier, while the Conservative Investor waits for lower risk levels to reenter.

This illustrates how RPT settings affect both exposure duration and performance outcomes.

Ironically, Buy & Hold investors or passive index fund investors are exposed to risk 100% of the time, enduring market crashes without the proactive risk management provided by the RISP 500™. With the RISP 500™, you gain the ability to navigate market ups and downs strategically, preserving capital while still capitalizing on favorable conditions.

The RISP 500 solution was designed to be super-easy to use and to take less than 1-5 min per day!

❶ Choose an RPT: Limit the highest X% of risks ever measured

What percentile of risks from 0 to 100% you are comfortable taking?

Example: If you choose 80%, you are accepting the 80% lowest risks and rejecting the top 20% highest risks

❷ Read the RISP 500™ Percentile every day

Subscribe the RISP 500™ Daily Live Readings

❸ Take Action on your stock portfolio

- If RISP 500 < RPT → Hold your stocks or risky assets (as you normally would)
- If RISP 500 > RPT → Seek protection (hedge), or sell risky assets to hold safe assets

You have 100% control: you choose RPT that fits your risk tolerance. Do it just one time. Adjust if necessary in the future. You choose your risky and safe assets (we can share ideas, if you like). We give you daily risk measurements: RISP 500.

6. The Science Behind the RISP 500 Methodology

The **RISP 500™** is calculated based on various data-driven metrics across different markets, including equity, volatility, bond, derivatives, and economic indicators. These indicators provide insights into market sentiment, risk levels, and economic outlook, allowing the RISP 500 to deliver a holistic risk measure. Below is a summary of each variable and its contribution to the RISP 500 model:

1. **Volatility Risk Premium (VRP):** Measures the difference between implied and actual volatility in the stock market, typically positive but can turn negative in times of high market stress. This shift indicates increased risk, as volatility expectations exceed historical levels.

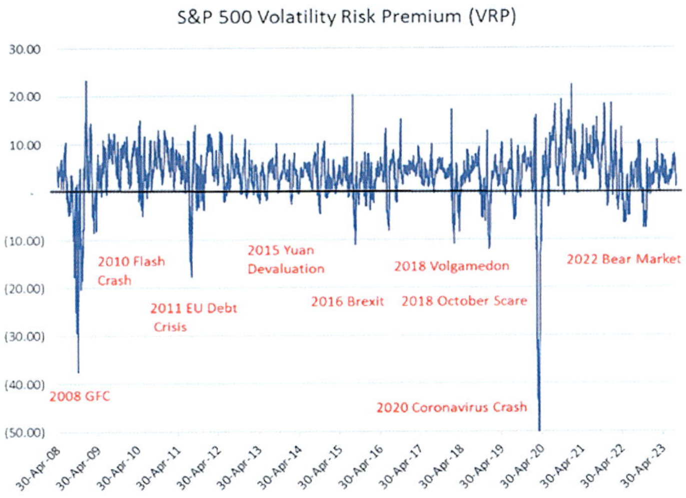

Volatility Risk Premium (VRP)	
	VRP > 0: Low risk in the stock market
	VRP < 0: High risk in the stock market

2. **VIX (Volatility Index):** The VIX represents expected S&P 500 volatility over the next 30 days and is widely viewed as a "fear gauge." Higher values signal rising risk and investor anxiety, while low values indicate market stability. Used with other metrics, the VIX helps assess shifts in market sentiment.

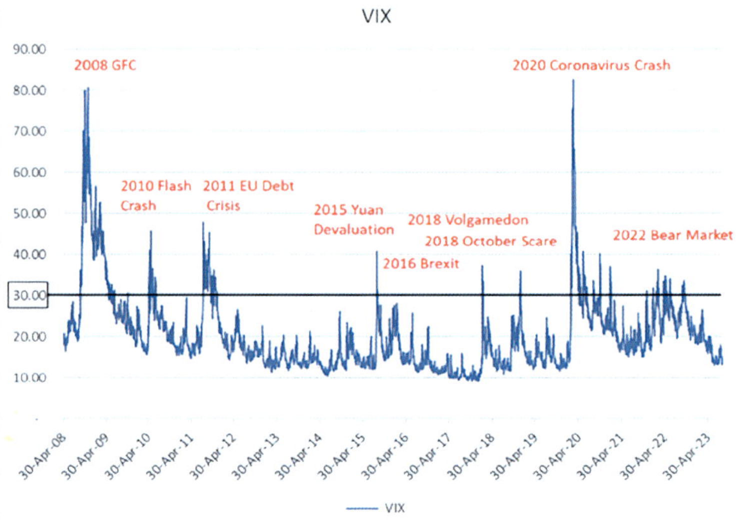

3. **VIX Cash Term Structure Curve:** The VIX term structure reflects volatility expectations over multiple time frames, from 9 days to 1 year. An upward-sloping curve is typical in calm markets, while a downward slope signals rising short-term risks. This structure offers quick insights into sentiment shifts across various time horizons.

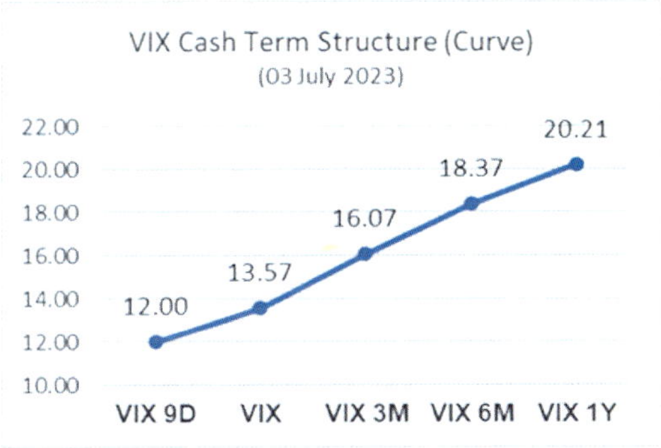

4. **VIX Futures Term Structure Curve:** Similar to the VIX Cash Term Structure, VIX futures show expected volatility across future dates. Upward slopes (contango) imply low-risk expectations, while downward slopes (backwardation) indicate market stress. This term structure assists in spotting risk trends and potential market shifts.

5. **Roll Yield:** Arising from the practice of rolling VIX futures contracts forward as they approach expiration, roll yield is positive in contango and negative in backwardation. This yield signals market stability when positive and heightened risk when negative, providing additional risk context.

VX1 < VIX → Positive Roll Yield → Contango → Safer market

VX1 > VIX → Negative Roll Yield → Backwardation → Riskier market

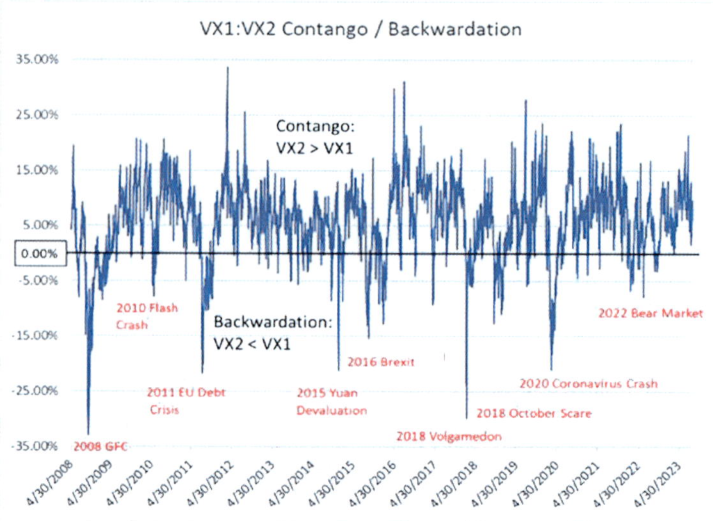

6. **VVIX (Volatility of VIX):** VVIX measures the expected volatility of the VIX itself, akin to "acceleration" in market volatility. A high VVIX indicates potential spikes in market turbulence, signaling heightened risk aversion and providing an added layer of risk analysis.

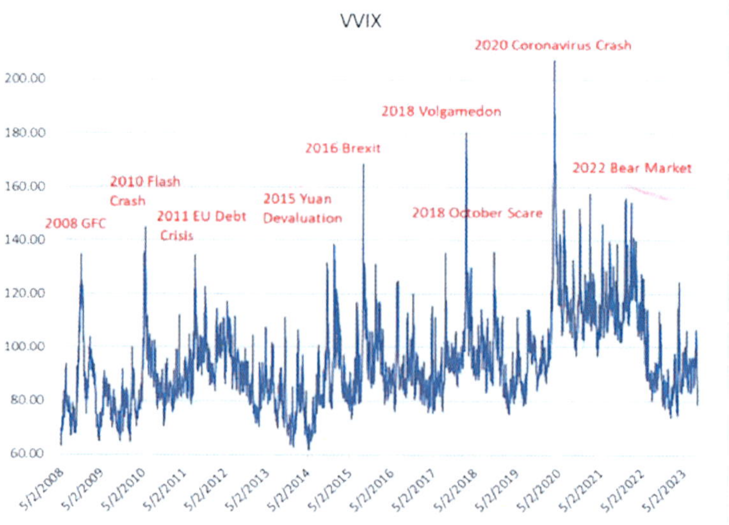

7. **Equity Risk Premium (ERP):** ERP represents the extra return investors expect from stocks over bonds to compensate for higher risk. When ERP narrows or turns negative, it suggests increased economic stress, making stocks less appealing relative to safer assets. ERP signals long-term risk conditions.

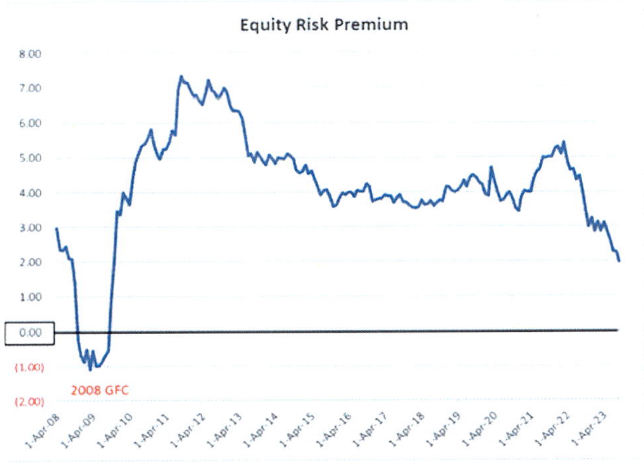

8. **Yield Curve Inversions:** Yield curve inversions (e.g., 10-year vs. 2-year Treasury yields) are historical indicators of recession, signaling market expectations of economic downturns. These inversions often coincide with stock market declines as investor risk appetite drops.

9. **MOVE Index (Bond Market Volatility):** The MOVE Index reflects expected volatility in U.S. Treasury bonds, with higher values signaling increased economic stress. Spikes in the MOVE Index often precede stock market declines, reflecting investor uncertainty about economic stability.

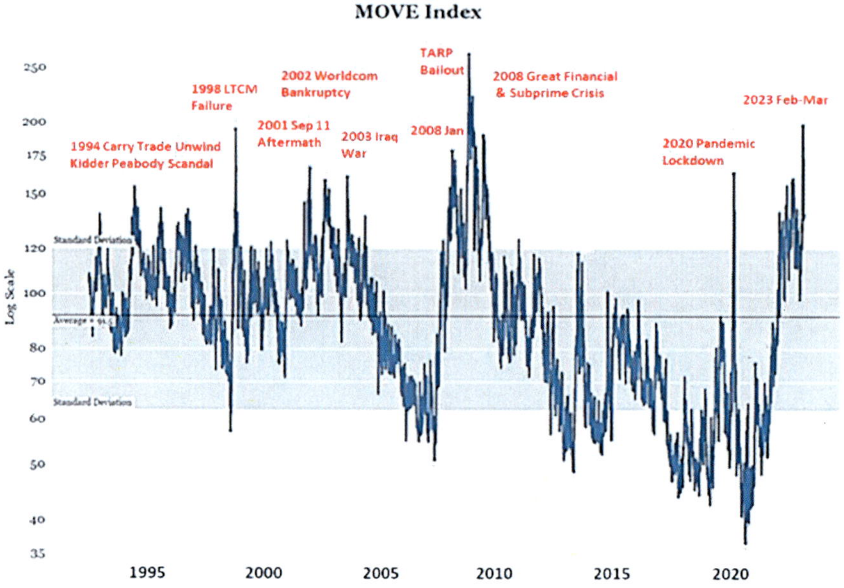

Credits: Bianco Research

10. **Leading Economic Indicators (LEI):** LEI, which comprises metrics like unemployment claims, stock prices, and building permits, provides early signals of economic turning points. LEI downturns often precede stock market declines, helping investors anticipate economic shifts.

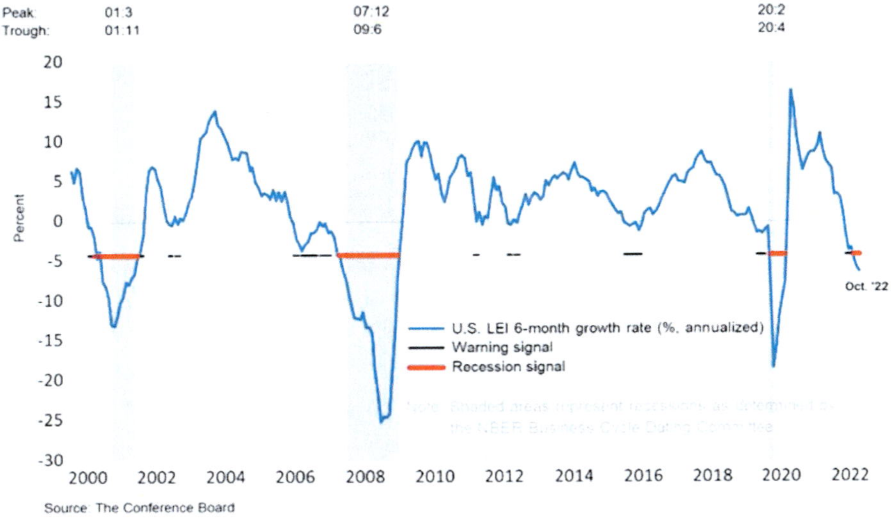

11. **Fed Policy and Rate Hike/Cut Probabilities:** Derived from Fed Funds Futures, this metric provides insight into market expectations for Federal Reserve rate decisions. Probabilities of rate changes reflect investor expectations for economic growth or contraction, influencing market volatility.

More than 15 variables are used in the determination of the RISP 500 indicator. We only showed 11 here. Each variable brings unique insights into the risk environment, contributing to the RISP 500's composite measure. By synthesizing these variables, the RISP 500 delivers a dynamic risk assessment tool, helping investors anticipate and respond to evolving market conditions.

7. Live Trading Results with RISP 500 (The Proof)

The RISP 500™ has been rigorously tested in live trading since January 1, 2022, delivering a comprehensive proof of concept. Guided by this tool, we've applied eight distinct strategies:

8 Strategies Tested Live

We tested 5 two-risk level and 3 three-risk level systems, totaling 8 strategies with 7 ETF assets and cash. For our tests, we selected the following assets:

THE RISP 500™ ASSET-RISK STRATEGY MATRIX

	Level of Risk (2)	Directional Asset		Leverage		Volatility
	HIGH	Cash	Cash	Cash	Cash	Cash
RISP 500™ at 75% percentile						
	LOW	SPY	QQQ	SSO	QLD	SVXY
		STRATEGY 1	STRATEGY 2	STRATEGY 3	STRATEGY 4	STRATEGY 5

	Level of Risk (3)	Based on S&P 500	Based on Nasdaq 100	Based on Volatility
	EXTREME	GLD	GLD	VIXM
RISP 500™ at 95% percentile				
	ELEVATED	SPY	QQQ	SPY
RISP 500™ at 70% percentile				
	LOW	SSO	QLD	SVXY
		STRATEGY 6	STRATEGY 7	STRATEGY 8

Risky Assets

SPY: ETF tracking the S&P 500® index

SSO: ETF tracking the S&P 500® index x2 (S&P 500® leveraged 2x)

QQQ: ETF tracking the Nasdaq 100 index

QLD: ETF tracking the Nasdaq 100 index x2 (Nasdaq 100 leveraged 2x)

SVXY: ETF tracking short VIX futures

Safe Assets

GLD: ETF tracking the price of gold
CASH

Long Volatility Asset (to explore high risk)
VIXM: ETF tracking long VIX futures

Strategy 1 (ST1-2L-SP500):
2-risk level strategy based on the S&P 500® (SPY/Cash)

Strategy 2 (ST2-2L-Nasdaq):
2-risk level strategy based on the Nasdaq 100 (QQQ/Cash)

Strategy 3 (ST3-2L-SP500x2):
2-risk level strategy based on the S&P 500® x2 (SSO/Cash)

Strategy 4 (ST4-2L-Nasdaqx2):
2-risk level strategy based on the Nasdaq 100 x2 (QLD/Cash)

Strategy 5 (ST5-2L-Volatility):
2-risk level strategy based on VIX Futures (QLD/Cash)

Strategy 6 (ST6-3L-SP500):
3-risk level strategy based on the S&P 500® (SSO/SPY/GLD)

Strategy 7 (ST7-3L-Nasdaq):
3-risk level strategy based on the Nasdaq 100 (QLD/QQQ/GLD)

Strategy 8 (ST8-3L-Volatility):
3-risk level strategy based on the VIX Futures (SVXY/SPY/VIXM)

We are constantly putting the RISP 500™ to the test and analyzing test results. We are also testing and back-testing new strategies all the time.

We are also making daily YTD and ITD performance results available on Facebook and X (formerly Twitter): www.facebook.com/risp500 and https://x.com/Risp500. As you know, every post on a social media platform has a date stamp, so you can trust the exact date and time we posted our daily performance results. Here's an example of a post:

DAILY TRADING BLOTTER & PERFORMANCE TRACKER

RISP 500™ Percentile Rank	37.6%

Date:	7/1/2024	Monday

Strategy 1: **ST-2L-SPY**
Assets: **SPY/Cash**

BUY	
HOLD	545.34
SELL	
RPT / STOP	75% / 3.0%
YTD Return	**16.42%**
Above S&P 500	+1.69%

Strategy 2: **ST-2L-QQQ**
Assets: **QQQ/Cash**

BUY	
HOLD	481.92
SELL	
RPT / STOP	75% / 5.5%
YTD Return	**21.77%**
Above S&P 500	+7.04%

Strategy 3: **ST-2L-SSO**
Assets: **SSO/Cash**

BUY	
HOLD	82.96
SELL	
RPT / STOP	75% / 9.0%
YTD Return	**31.66%**
Above S&P 500	+16.92%

Strategy 4: **ST-2L-QLD**
Assets: **QLD/Cash**

BUY	
HOLD	101.03
SELL	
RPT / STOP	75% / 11.5%
YTD Return	**42.88%**
Above S&P 500	+28.15%

Strategy 5: **ST-2L-SVXY**
Assets: **SVXY/Cash**

BUY	
HOLD	62.55
SELL	
RPT / STOP	75% / 8.5%
YTD Return	**16.42%**
Above S&P 500	+1.69%

Strategy 6: **ST-3L-SP500**
Assets: **SSO/SPY/GLD**

BUY		
HOLD	82.60	SSO
SELL		
RPT-1/ RPT-2	70%	95%
YTD Return	**25.93%**	
Above S&P 500	+11.20%	

Strategy 7: **ST-3L-Nasdaq**
Assets: **QLD/QQQ/GLD**

BUY		
HOLD	99.81	QLD
SELL		
RPT-1/ RPT-2	70%	95%
YTD Return	**30.82%**	
Above S&P 500	+16.09%	

Strategy 8: **ST-3L-Volatility**
Assets: **SVXY/SPY/VIXM**

BUY		
HOLD	61.39	SVXY
SELL		
RPT-1/ RPT-2	70%	96%
YTD Return	**18.39%**	
Above S&P 500	+3.65%	

* **Gain: YTD excess return above S&P 500**
Correlation: Strategy with S&P 500
SPY: ETF tracking the S&P 500 index
SSO: ETF tracking the S&P 500 index x2
QQQ: ETF tracking the Nasdaq 100 index
QLD: ETF tracking the Nasdaq 100 index x2
SVXY: ETF tracking short VIX futures
VIXM: ETF tracking long VIX futures
GLD: ETF tracking the price of Gold

2024 YTD Return Ranking

Asset/Strategy	YTD Return
ST-2L-Nasdaqx2	**42.88%**
QLD	32.93%
ST-2L-SP500x2	**31.66%**
ST-3L-Nasdaq	**30.82%**
SSO	27.49%
ST-3L-SP500	**25.93%**
ST-2L-Nasdaq	**21.77%**
SVXY	20.99%
ST-3L-Volatility	**18.39%**
QQQ	17.68%
ST-2L-SP500	**16.42%**
ST-2L-Volatility	**16.42%**
SPY (S&P 500)	**14.73%**

Published every day after the close

2022 to Date Performance Ranking 7/1/2024

Asset/Strategy	Cum. Return	CAGR	Max DD	RoMaD
ST-3L-Volatility	**210.17%**	56.26%	**-14.88%**	**14.1x**
ST-3L-Nasdaq	**209.75%**	56.17%	**-22.78%**	**9.2x**
ST-2L-Volatility	**207.66%**	55.70%	**-21.16%**	**9.8x**
ST-2L-Nasdaqx2	**183.33%**	50.78%	**-31.70%**	**5.8x**
ST-3L-SP500	**177.22%**	49.49%	**-15.75%**	**11.3x**
ST-2L-SP500x2	**121.19%**	36.76%	**-18.58%**	**6.5x**
SVXY	103.25%	32.27%	-28.46%	3.6x
ST-2L-Nasdaq	**77.84%**	25.48%	**-14.52%**	**5.4x**
ST-2L-SP500	**55.81%**	19.11%	**-8.72%**	**6.4x**
QQQ	21.13%	7.85%	-35.59%	0.6x
SPY (S&P 500)	**14.82%**	**5.60%**	**-25.51%**	**0.6x**
QLD	13.49%	5.12%	-64.50%	0.2x
SSO	13.36%	5.07%	-47.32%	0.3x

Max DD: Maximum Drawdowns, RoMaD: Return over Maxium Drawdowns

THE RISP 500™ ASSET-RISK STRATEGY MATRIX

Level of Risk (2)	Directional Asset		Leverage		Volatility
HIGH (RISP 500™ at 75% percentile)	Cash	Cash	Cash	Cash	Cash
LOW	SPY	QQQ	SSO	QLD	SVXY
	STRATEGY 1	STRATEGY 2	STRATEGY 3	STRATEGY 4	STRATEGY 5

Level of Risk (3)	Based on S&P 500	Based on Nasdaq 100	Based on Volatility
EXTREME (RISP 500™ at 95% percentile)	GLD	GLD	VIXM
ELEVATED (RISP 500™ at 70% percentile)	SPY	QQQ	SPY
LOW	SSO	QLD	SVXY
	STRATEGY 6	STRATEGY 7	STRATEGY 8

RISP 500™ measured 1x a day is already sufficient for strong long-term results

In this project, we are reading the RISP 500™ only once a day to **prove that even with a single reading a day will be enough to deliver strong results**. We take the official measurement of the day's RISP 500™ between 10:00 a.m. and 2:00 pm (New York time/ET).

We actually measure the RISP 500™ all day long, even during pre-market and post-market hours, which is even more powerful as a live, real-time indicator. But results show that long-term investors are able to achieve the above results with just one RISP 500™ reading a day. Because of low turnover, in most days, there will be no trades at all, which is perfect for most investors and wealth management professionals alike.

KEY RESULTS FROM LIVE TRADING OF THE 8 STRATEGIES

Outperformance Across All Strategies

Over 2 ½ years of live trading (January 2022–July 2024), **all eight strategies outperformed the S&P 500®**, even during the challenging 2022 bear market. **Leveraged and volatility-based strategies delivered particularly strong results in both bear and bull markets**, demonstrating SMIGRM's adaptability to varying market conditions.

Significantly Reduced Drawdowns

While the S&P 500® experienced a maximum drawdown of -25.51% during the 2022 bear market, **SMIGRM strategies experienced lower drawdowns, helping preserve capital during volatile periods**. This ability to sidestep the worst market downturns is a hallmark of the RISP 500™'s effectiveness.

Hugely Enhanced Return-to-Risk Ratio

SMIGRM strategies consistently achieved higher RoMaD ratios compared to the S&P 500®, indicating **superior returns for the risks taken**. By avoiding high-risk periods and capitalizing on favorable conditions, the RISP 500™ has proven its value as a risk-management and performance-enhancement tool.

Real Results with Transparency

All live trading results are shared daily on Facebook and X (formerly Twitter), ensuring full transparency. This allows wealth managers and investors to monitor the RISP 500™'s performance and validate its effectiveness daily: www.facebook.com/risp500 or https://x.com/Risp500.

The Bottom Line

SMIGRM, powered by the RISP 500™, transforms wealth management. Whether avoiding the 2022 bear market's worst losses or outperforming during subsequent rallies, it consistently proves its ability to protect and grow wealth. By leveraging this system, you can offer clients unmatched performance and peace of mind in any market environment.

By the time of this writing, all 8 strategies have performed above expectations in live trading. We have chosen a RPT of 75% for all 5 two-risk level strategies. For the three-risk level strategies, we have chosen RPT-1 at 70% and RPT-2 at 95%.

The following charts illustrate the growth of $1,000 from 1/1/2022 to 7/1/2024 and drawdowns experienced during the period.

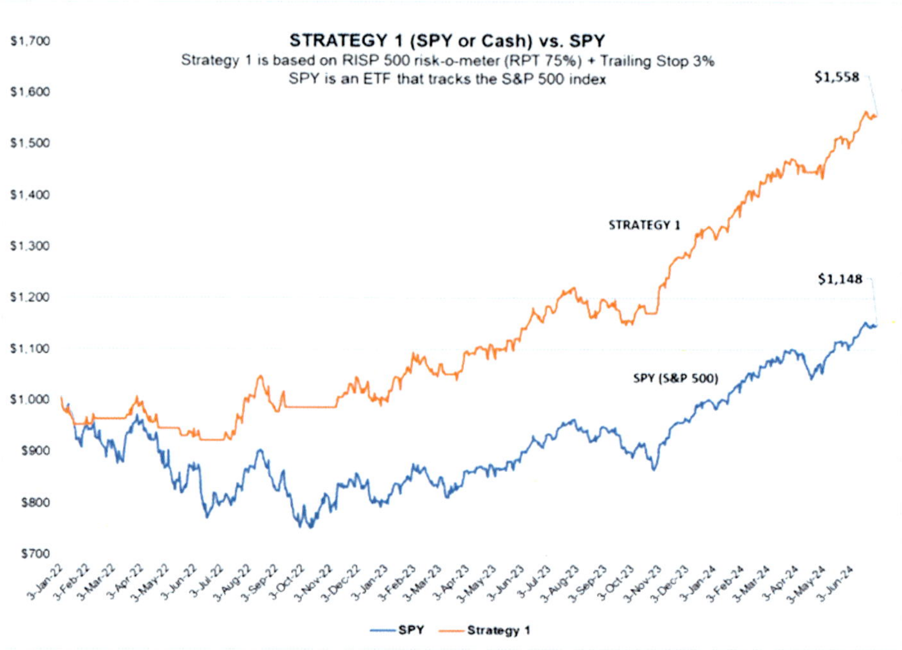
STRATEGY 1 (SPY or Cash) vs. SPY
Strategy 1 is based on RISP 500 risk-o-meter (RPT 75%) + Trailing Stop 3%
SPY is an ETF that tracks the S&P 500 index
$1,558
STRATEGY 1
$1,148
SPY (S&P 500)
$1,700
$1,600
$1,500
$1,400
$1,300
$1,200
$1,100
$1,000
$900
$800
$700
SPY
Strategy 1

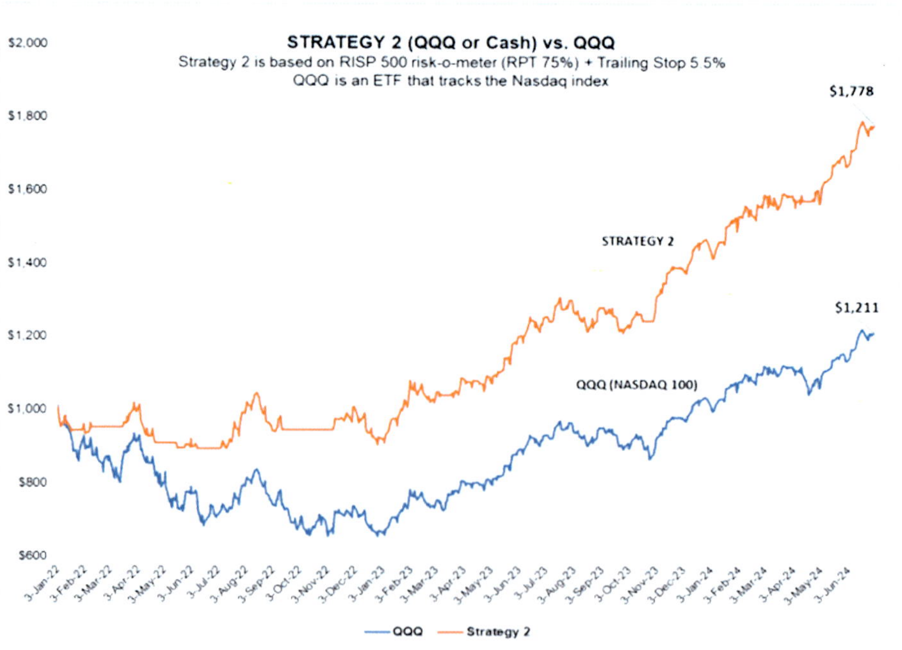
STRATEGY 2 (QQQ or Cash) vs. QQQ
Strategy 2 is based on RISP 500 risk-o-meter (RPT 75%) + Trailing Stop 5.5%
QQQ is an ETF that tracks the Nasdaq index
$1,778
STRATEGY 2
$1,211
QQQ (NASDAQ 100)
$2,000
$1,800
$1,600
$1,400
$1,200
$1,000
$800
$600
QQQ
Strategy 2

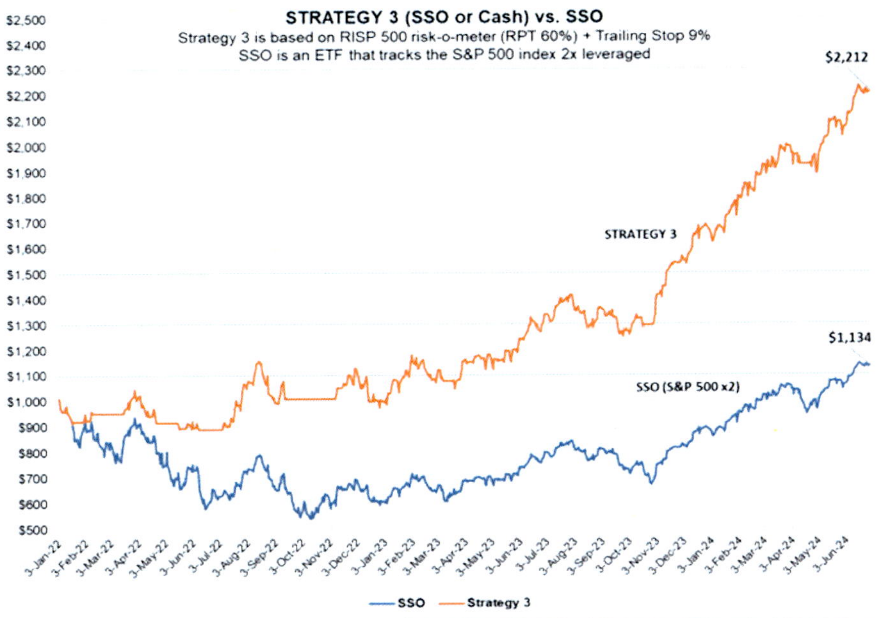

STRATEGY 3 (SSO or Cash) vs. SSO
Strategy 3 is based on RISP 500 risk-o-meter (RPT 60%) + Trailing Stop 9%
SSO is an ETF that tracks the S&P 500 index 2x leveraged
$2,212
STRATEGY 3
$1,134
SSO (S&P 500 x2)
$2,500
$2,400
$2,300
$2,200
$2,100
$2,000
$1,900
$1,800
$1,700
$1,600
$1,500
$1,400
$1,300
$1,200
$1,100
$1,000
$900
$800
$700
$600
$500
3-Jan-22
3-Feb-22
3-Mar-22
3-Apr-22
3-May-22
3-Jun-22
3-Jul-22
3-Aug-22
3-Sep-22
3-Oct-22
3-Nov-22
3-Dec-22
3-Jan-23
3-Feb-23
3-Mar-23
3-Apr-23
3-May-23
3-Jun-23
3-Jul-23
3-Aug-23
3-Sep-23
3-Oct-23
3-Nov-23
3-Dec-23
3-Jan-24
3-Feb-24
3-Mar-24
3-Apr-24
3-May-24
3-Jun-24
SSO
Strategy 3

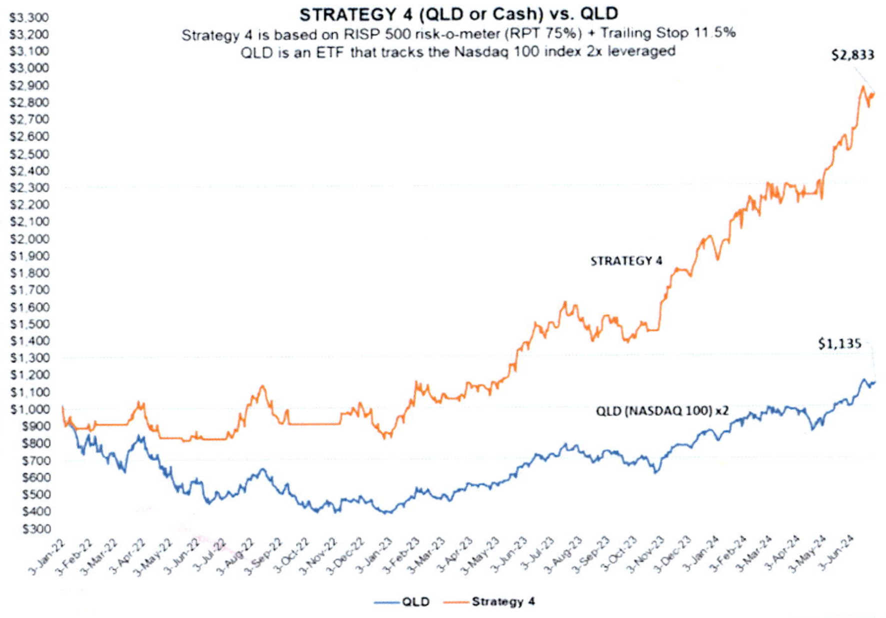

STRATEGY 4 (QLD or Cash) vs. QLD
Strategy 4 is based on RISP 500 risk-o-meter (RPT 75%) + Trailing Stop 11.5%
QLD is an ETF that tracks the Nasdaq 100 index 2x leveraged
$2,833
STRATEGY 4
$1,135
QLD (NASDAQ 100) x2
$3,300
$3,200
$3,100
$3,000
$2,900
$2,800
$2,700
$2,600
$2,500
$2,400
$2,300
$2,200
$2,100
$2,000
$1,900
$1,800
$1,700
$1,600
$1,500
$1,400
$1,300
$1,200
$1,100
$1,000
$900
$800
$700
$600
$500
$400
$300
3-Jan-22
3-Feb-22
3-Mar-22
3-Apr-22
3-May-22
3-Jun-22
3-Jul-22
3-Aug-22
3-Sep-22
3-Oct-22
3-Nov-22
3-Dec-22
3-Jan-23
3-Feb-23
3-Mar-23
3-Apr-23
3-May-23
3-Jun-23
3-Jul-23
3-Aug-23
3-Sep-23
3-Oct-23
3-Nov-23
3-Dec-23
3-Jan-24
3-Feb-24
3-Mar-24
3-Apr-24
3-May-24
3-Jun-24
QLD
Strategy 4

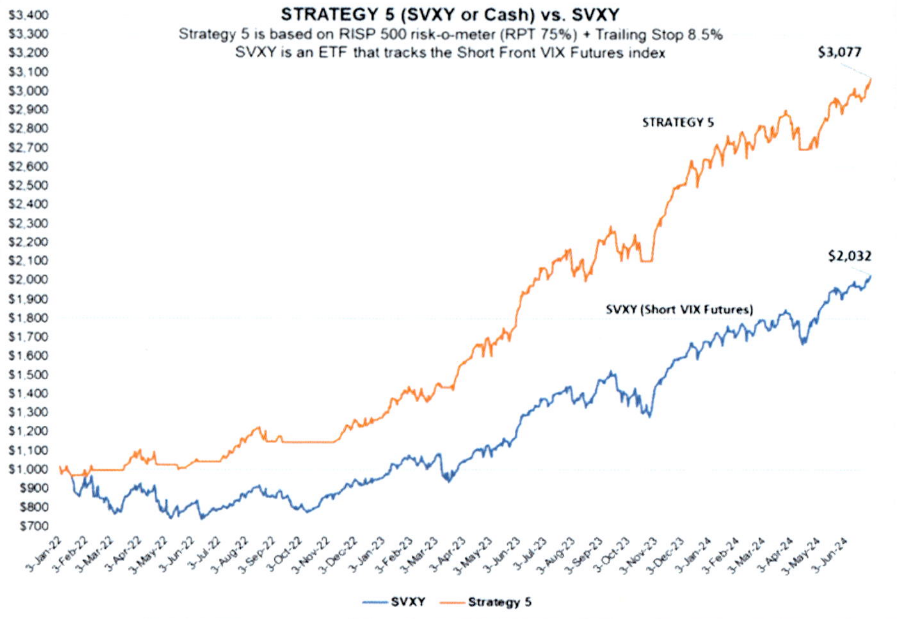
STRATEGY 5 (SVXY or Cash) vs. SVXY
Strategy 5 is based on RISP 500 risk-o-meter (RPT 75%) + Trailing Stop 8.5%
SVXY is an ETF that tracks the Short Front VIX Futures index
$3,077
STRATEGY 5
$2,032
SVXY (Short VIX Futures)
SVXY
Strategy 5

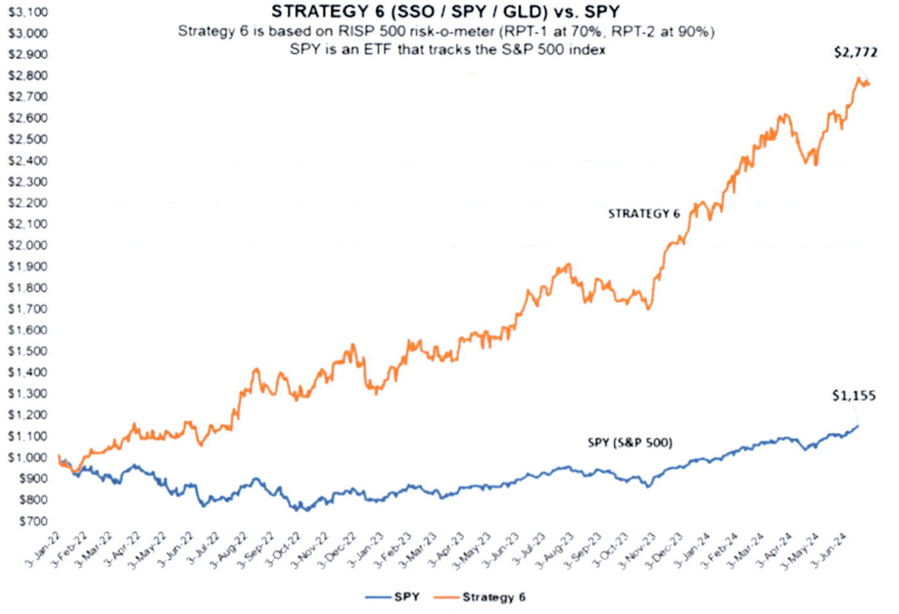
STRATEGY 6 (SSO / SPY / GLD) vs. SPY
Strategy 6 is based on RISP 500 risk-o-meter (RPT-1 at 70%, RPT-2 at 90%)
SPY is an ETF that tracks the S&P 500 index
$2,772
STRATEGY 6
$1,155
SPY (S&P 500)
SPY
Strategy 6

STRATEGY 7 (QLD / QQQ / GLD) vs. QQQ
Strategy 7 is based on RISP 500 risk-o-meter (RPT-1 at 70%, RPT-2 at 90%)
QQQ is an ETF that tracks the NASDAQ 100 index
$3,098
STRATEGY 6
$1,211
QQQ (NASDAQ 100)
QQQ
Strategy 7

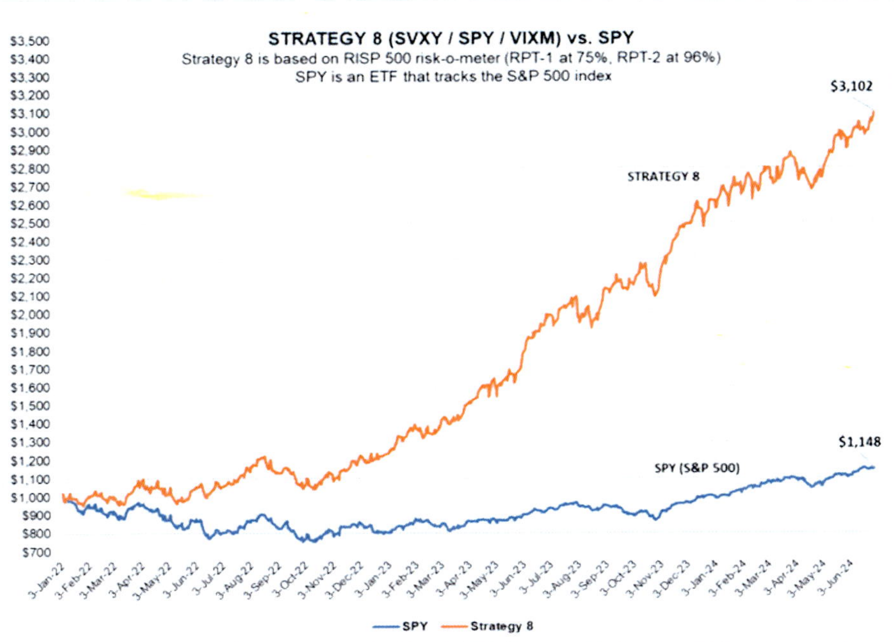
STRATEGY 8 (SVXY / SPY / VIXM) vs. SPY
Strategy 8 is based on RISP 500 risk-o-meter (RPT-1 at 75%, RPT-2 at 96%)
SPY is an ETF that tracks the S&P 500 index
$3,102
STRATEGY 8
$1,148
SPY (S&P 500)
SPY
Strategy 8

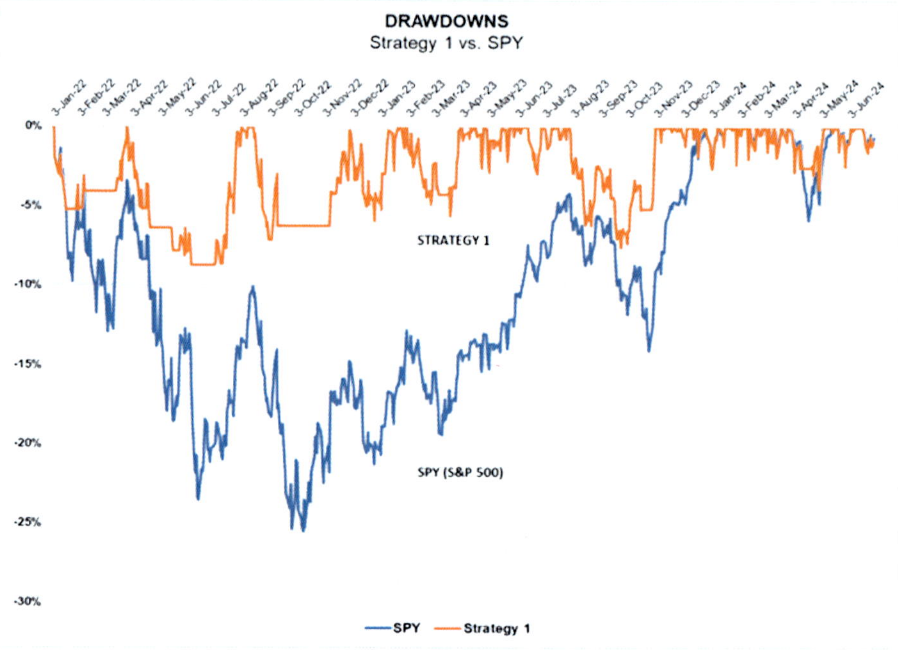
DRAWDOWNS
Strategy 1 vs. SPY
STRATEGY 1
SPY (S&P 500)
0%
-5%
-10%
-15%
-20%
-25%
-30%
SPY
Strategy 1

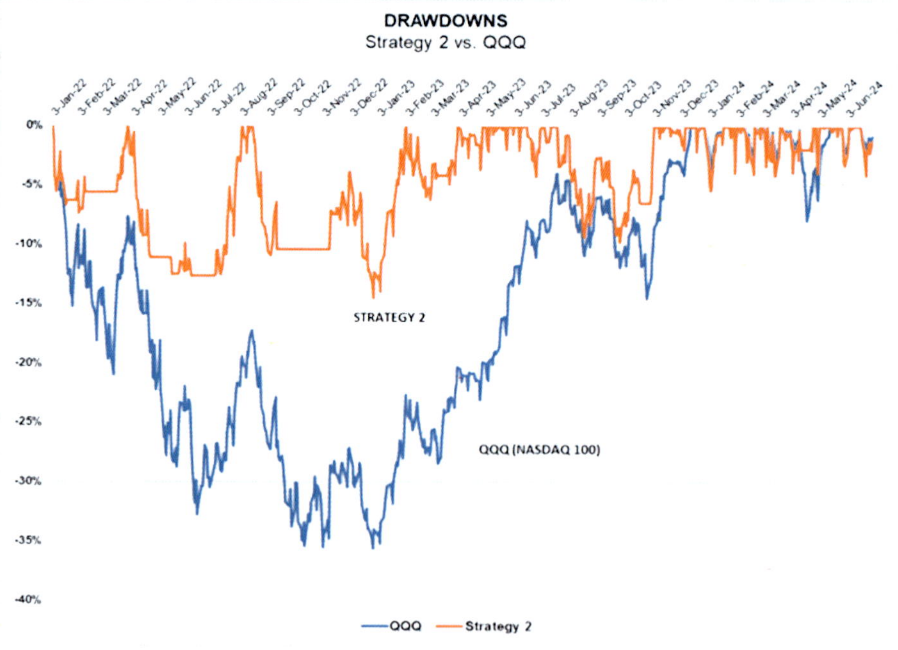
DRAWDOWNS
Strategy 2 vs. QQQ
STRATEGY 2
QQQ (NASDAQ 100)
0%
-5%
-10%
-15%
-20%
-25%
-30%
-35%
-40%
QQQ
Strategy 2

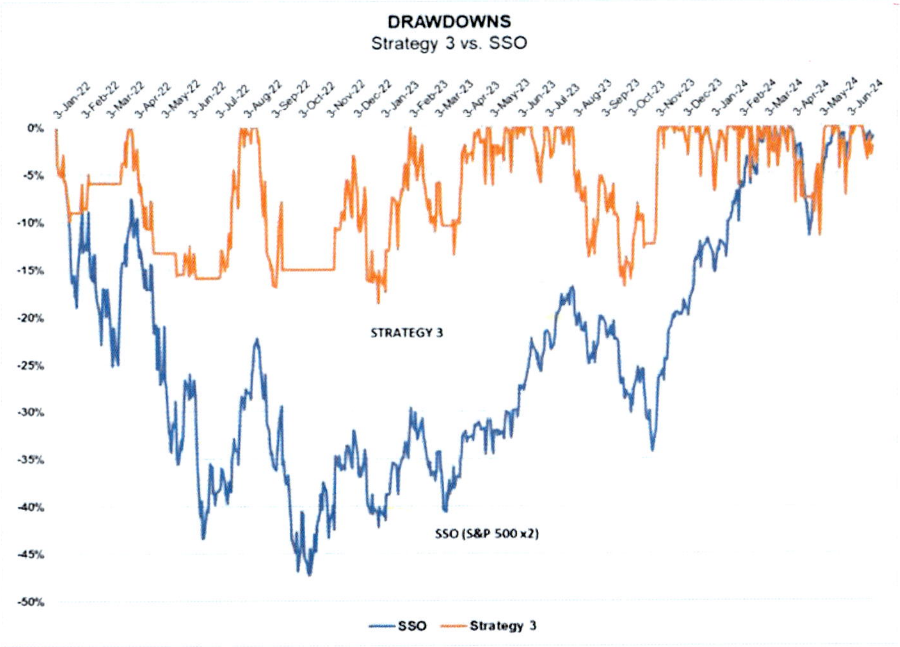
DRAWDOWNS
Strategy 3 vs. SSO
3-Jan-22
3-Feb-22
3-Mar-22
3-Apr-22
3-May-22
3-Jun-22
3-Jul-22
3-Aug-22
3-Sep-22
3-Oct-22
3-Nov-22
3-Dec-22
3-Jan-23
3-Feb-23
3-Mar-23
3-Apr-23
3-May-23
3-Jun-23
3-Jul-23
3-Aug-23
3-Sep-23
3-Oct-23
3-Nov-23
3-Dec-23
3-Jan-24
3-Feb-24
3-Mar-24
3-Apr-24
3-May-24
3-Jun-24
0%
-5%
-10%
-15%
-20%
-25%
-30%
-35%
-40%
-45%
-50%
STRATEGY 3
SSO (S&P 500 x2)
SSO
Strategy 3

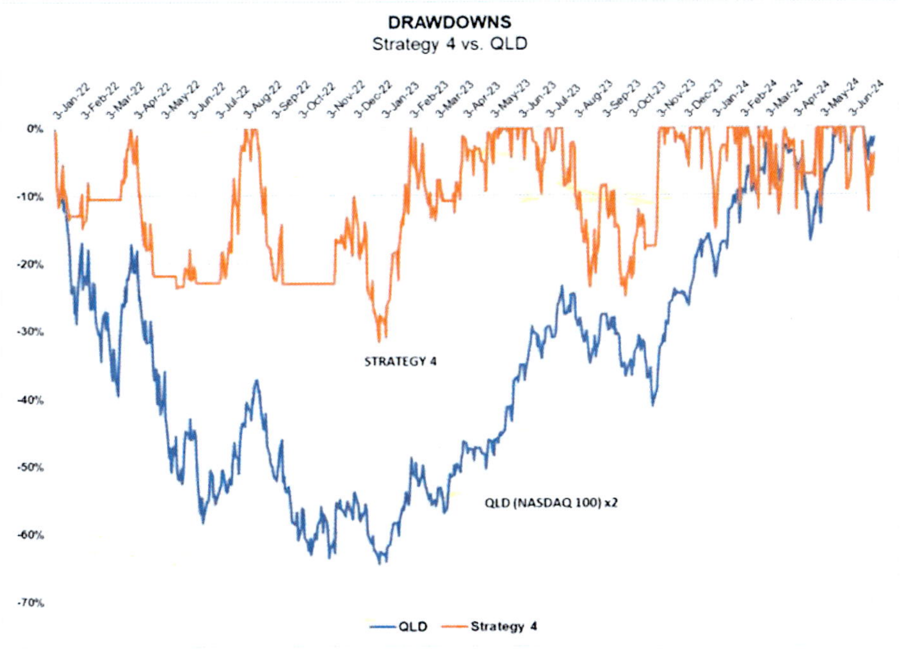
DRAWDOWNS
Strategy 4 vs. QLD
3-Jan-22
3-Feb-22
3-Mar-22
3-Apr-22
3-May-22
3-Jun-22
3-Jul-22
3-Aug-22
3-Sep-22
3-Oct-22
3-Nov-22
3-Dec-22
3-Jan-23
3-Feb-23
3-Mar-23
3-Apr-23
3-May-23
3-Jun-23
3-Jul-23
3-Aug-23
3-Sep-23
3-Oct-23
3-Nov-23
3-Dec-23
3-Jan-24
3-Feb-24
3-Mar-24
3-Apr-24
3-May-24
3-Jun-24
0%
-10%
-20%
-30%
-40%
-50%
-60%
-70%
STRATEGY 4
QLD (NASDAQ 100) x2
QLD
Strategy 4

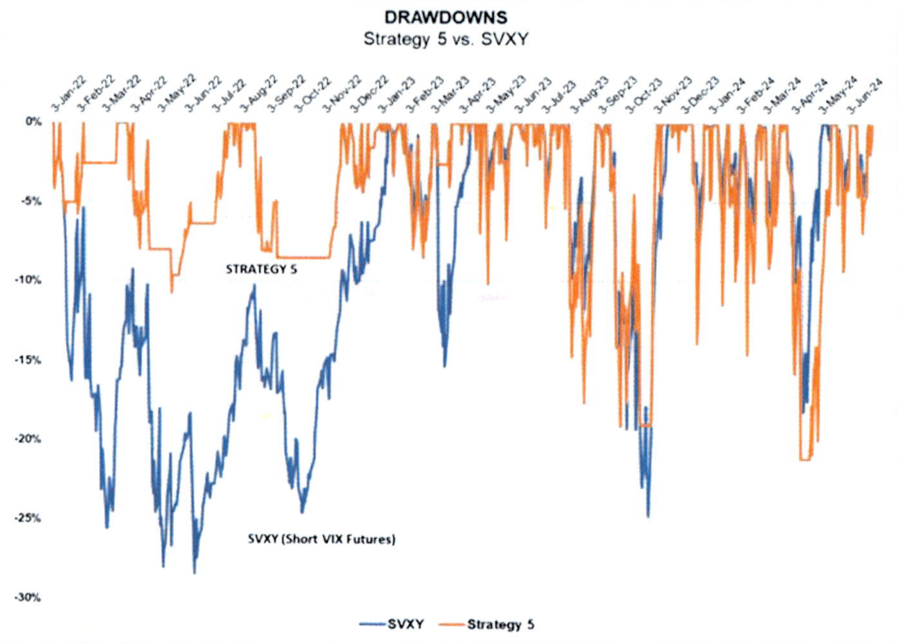
DRAWDOWNS
Strategy 5 vs. SVXY
3-Jan-22
3-Feb-22
3-Mar-22
3-Apr-22
3-May-22
3-Jun-22
3-Jul-22
3-Aug-22
3-Sep-22
3-Oct-22
3-Nov-22
3-Dec-22
3-Jan-23
3-Feb-23
3-Mar-23
3-Apr-23
3-May-23
3-Jun-23
3-Jul-23
3-Aug-23
3-Sep-23
3-Oct-23
3-Nov-23
3-Dec-23
3-Jan-24
3-Feb-24
3-Mar-24
3-Apr-24
3-May-24
3-Jun-24
0%
-5%
-10%
-15%
-20%
-25%
-30%
STRATEGY 5
SVXY (Short VIX Futures)
SVXY
Strategy 5

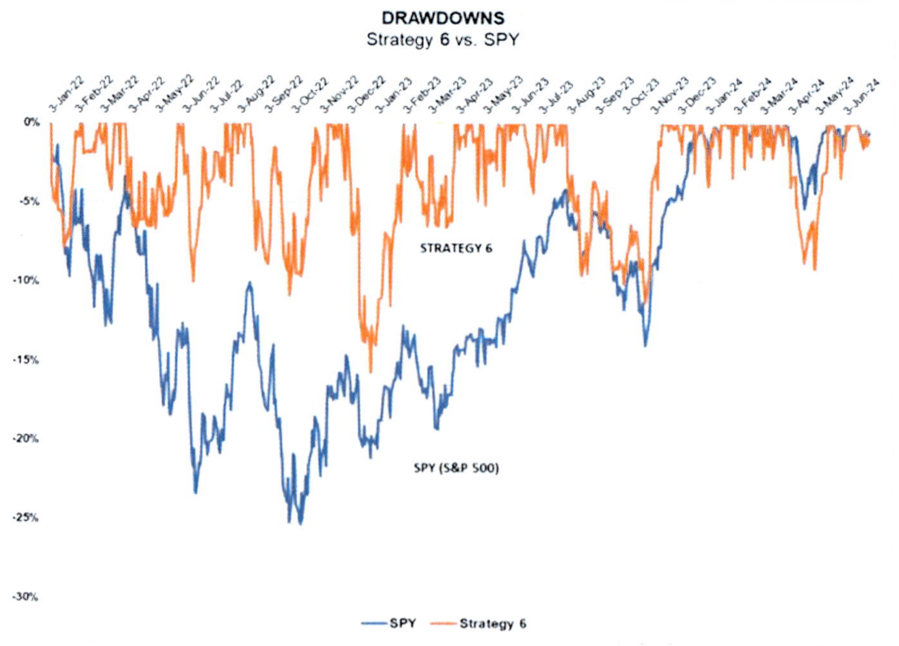
DRAWDOWNS
Strategy 6 vs. SPY
3-Jan-22
3-Feb-22
3-Mar-22
3-Apr-22
3-May-22
3-Jun-22
3-Jul-22
3-Aug-22
3-Sep-22
3-Oct-22
3-Nov-22
3-Dec-22
3-Jan-23
3-Feb-23
3-Mar-23
3-Apr-23
3-May-23
3-Jun-23
3-Jul-23
3-Aug-23
3-Sep-23
3-Oct-23
3-Nov-23
3-Dec-23
3-Jan-24
3-Feb-24
3-Mar-24
3-Apr-24
3-May-24
3-Jun-24
0%
-5%
-10%
-15%
-20%
-25%
-30%
STRATEGY 6
SPY (S&P 500)
SPY
Strategy 6

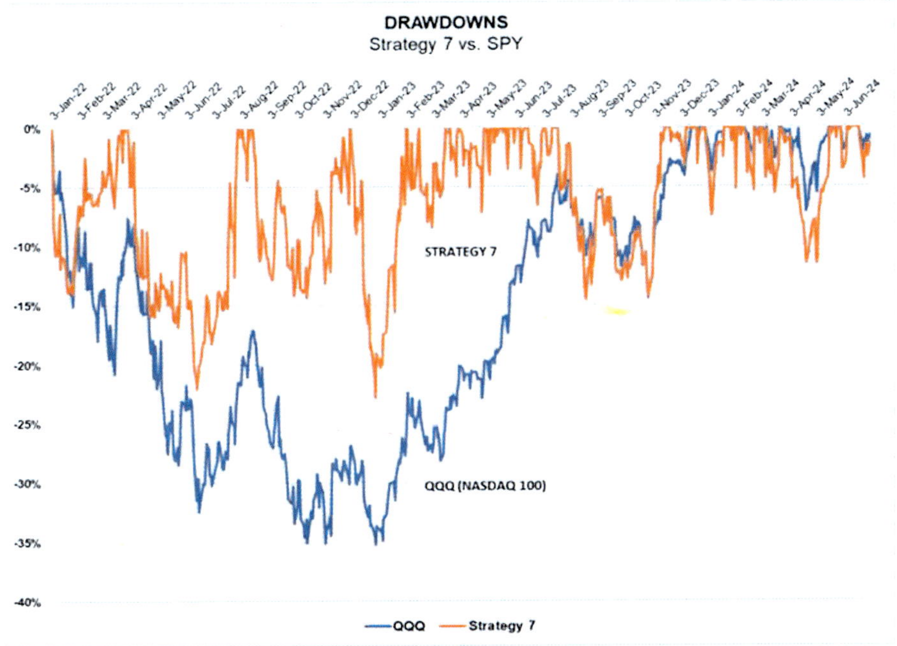
DRAWDOWNS
Strategy 7 vs. SPY
3-Jan-22
3-Feb-22
3-Mar-22
3-Apr-22
3-May-22
3-Jun-22
3-Jul-22
3-Aug-22
3-Sep-22
3-Oct-22
3-Nov-22
3-Dec-22
3-Jan-23
3-Feb-23
3-Mar-23
3-Apr-23
3-May-23
3-Jun-23
3-Jul-23
3-Aug-23
3-Sep-23
3-Oct-23
3-Nov-23
3-Dec-23
3-Jan-24
3-Feb-24
3-Mar-24
3-Apr-24
3-May-24
3-Jun-24
0%
-5%
-10%
-15%
-20%
-25%
-30%
-35%
-40%
STRATEGY 7
QQQ (NASDAQ 100)
QQQ
Strategy 7

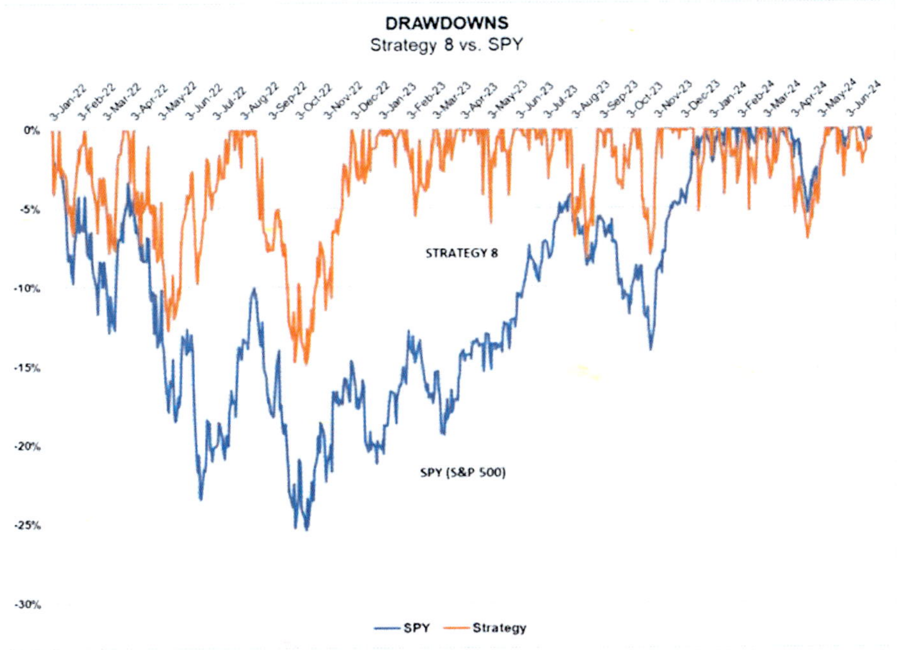
DRAWDOWNS
Strategy 8 vs. SPY
3-Jan-22
3-Feb-22
3-Mar-22
3-Apr-22
3-May-22
3-Jun-22
3-Jul-22
3-Aug-22
3-Sep-22
3-Oct-22
3-Nov-22
3-Dec-22
3-Jan-23
3-Feb-23
3-Mar-23
3-Apr-23
3-May-23
3-Jun-23
3-Jul-23
3-Aug-23
3-Sep-23
3-Oct-23
3-Nov-23
3-Dec-23
3-Jan-24
3-Feb-24
3-Mar-24
3-Apr-24
3-May-24
3-Jun-24
0%
-5%
-10%
-15%
-20%
-25%
-30%
STRATEGY 8
SPY (S&P 500)
SPY
Strategy

2022 to Date Performance Ranking 1-Jul-2024

Asset/Strategy	Cum. Return	CAGR	Max DD	RoMaD
ST8-3L-Volatility	210.17%	56.26%	-14.88%	14.1x
ST7-3L-Nasdaq	209.75%	56.17%	-22.78%	9.2x
ST5-2L-Volatility	207.66%	55.76%	-21.16%	9.8x
ST4-2L-Nasdaqx2	183.33%	50.78%	-31.70%	5.8x
ST6-3L-SP500	177.22%	49.49%	-15.75%	11.3x
ST3-2L-SP500x2	121.19%	36.76%	-18.58%	6.5x
SVXY	103.25%	32.27%	-28.46%	3.6x
ST2-2L-Nasdaq	77.84%	25.48%	-14.52%	5.4x
ST1-2L-SP500	55.81%	19.11%	-8.72%	6.4x
QQQ	21.13%	7.85%	-35.59%	0.6x
SPY (S&P 500)	14.82%	5.60%	-25.51%	0.6x
QLD	13.49%	5.12%	-64.50%	0.2x
SSO	13.36%	5.07%	-47.32%	0.3x

Max DD: Maximum Drawdowns, RoMaD: Return over Maximum Drawdowns
Since 01 Jan 2022. Cumulative return is compounded daily.

How Much Has $1,000 On 01/Jan/2022 Turned Into:

Asset/Strategy	Amount on 01/Jul/2024
ST-3L-Volatility	$3,101.70
ST-3L-Nasdaq	$3,097.52
ST-2L-Volatility	$3,076.62
ST-2L-Nasdaqx2	$2,833.30
ST-3L-SP500	$2,772.24
ST-2L-SP500x2	$2,211.92
SVXY (VIX Futures)	$2,032.49
ST-2L-Nasdaq	$1,778.39
ST-2L-SP500	$1,558.15
QQQ (Nasdaq 100)	$1,211.31
SPY (S&P 500)	$1,148.18
QLD (Nasdaq 100 x2)	$1,134.91
SSO (S&P 500 x2)	$1,133.57

2022 - 2024 YTD ANNUAL PERFORMANCE CONTROL 1-Jul-2024

Year	S&P 500 Annual Return	STRATEGY 1 Annual Return	Gain over S&P 500	STRATEGY 2 Annual Return	Gain over S&P 500
2022	-19.48%	0.53%	20.01%	-7.61%	11.87%
2023	24.29%	33.13%	8.84%	58.07%	33.78%
YTD 2024	14.73%	16.42%	+1.69%	21.77%	+7.04%

Year	S&P 500 Annual Return	STRATEGY 3 Annual Return	Gain over S&P 500	STRATEGY 4 Annual Return	Gain over S&P 500
2022	-19.48%	0.18%	19.66%	-14.32%	5.16%
2023	24.29%	67.71%	43.42%	131.44%	107.15%
YTD 2024	14.73%	31.66%	+16.92%	42.88%	+28.15%

Year	S&P 500 Annual Return	STRATEGY 5 Annual Return	Gain over S&P 500	STRATEGY 6 Annual Return	Gain over S&P 500
2022	-19.48%	27.33%	46.81%	33.42%	52.91%
2023	24.29%	107.55%	83.26%	64.99%	40.71%
YTD 2024	14.73%	16.42%	+1.69%	25.93%	+11.20%

Year	S&P 500 Annual Return	STRATEGY 7 Annual Return	Gain over S&P 500	STRATEGY 8 Annual Return	Gain over S&P 500
2022	-19.48%	2.37%	21.85%	22.99%	42.47%
2023	24.29%	131.29%	107.00%	113.02%	88.73%
YTD 2024	14.73%	30.82%	+16.09%	18.39%	+3.65%

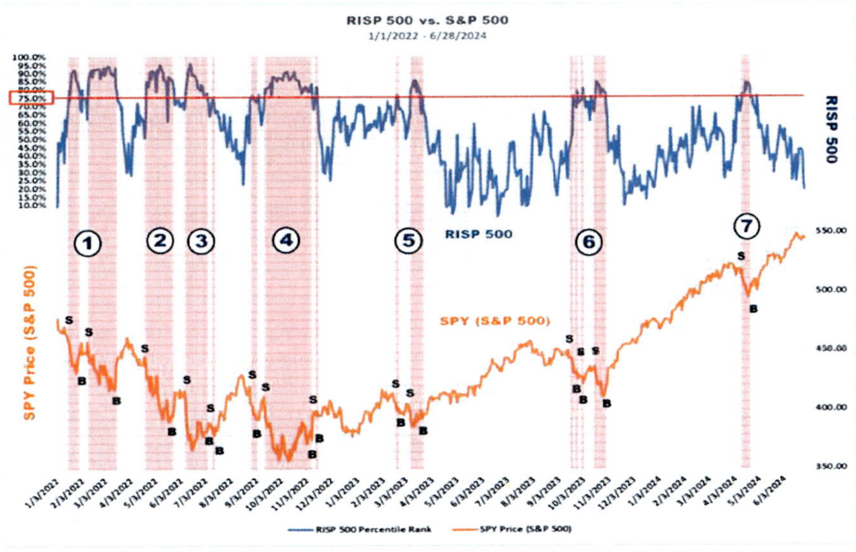
RISP 500 vs. S&P 500
1/1/2022 - 6/28/2024
RISP 500
SPY (S&P 500)
SPY Price (S&P 500)
RISP 500 Percentile Rank
SPY Price (S&P 500)

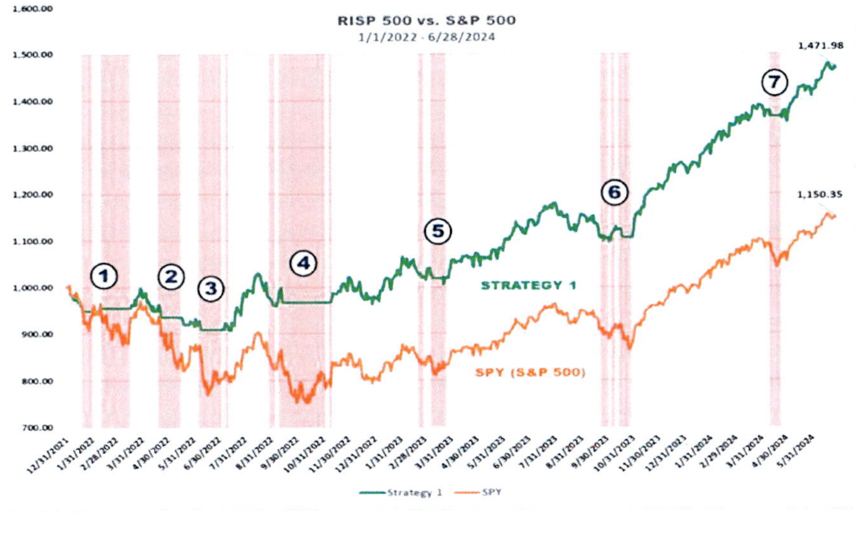
RISP 500 vs. S&P 500
1/1/2022 - 6/28/2024
1,471.98
1,150.35
STRATEGY 1
SPY (S&P 500)
Strategy 1
SPY

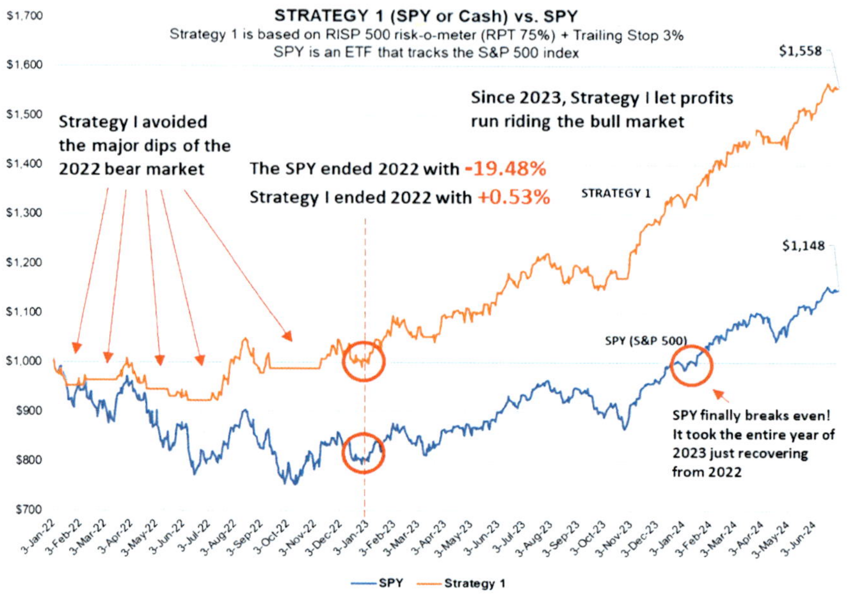
STRATEGY 1 (SPY or Cash) vs. SPY
Strategy 1 is based on RISP 500 risk-o-meter (RPT 75%) + Trailing Stop 3%
SPY is an ETF that tracks the S&P 500 index
Strategy I avoided the major dips of the 2022 bear market
The SPY ended 2022 with -19.48%
Strategy I ended 2022 with +0.53%
Since 2023, Strategy I let profits run riding the bull market
STRATEGY 1
$1,558
$1,148
SPY (S&P 500)
SPY finally breaks even! It took the entire year of 2023 just recovering from 2022
SPY
Strategy 1

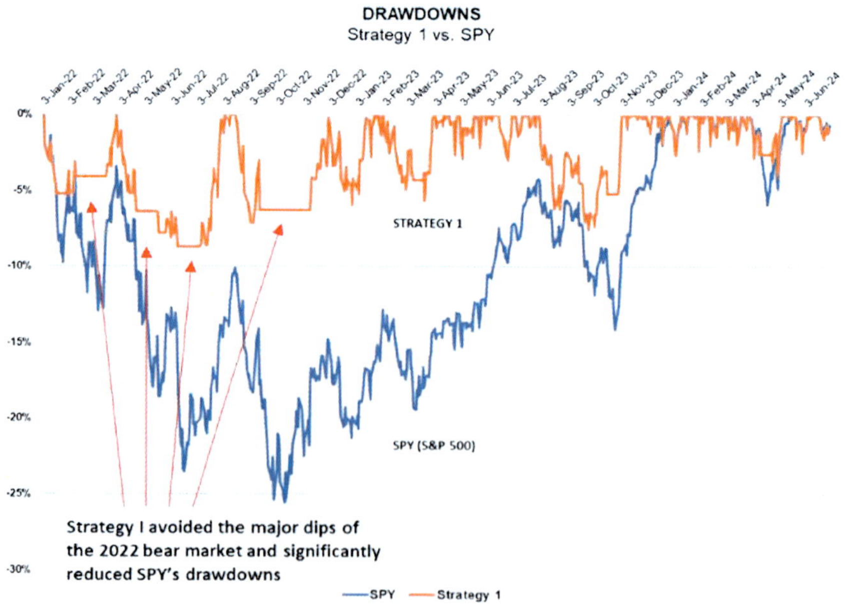
DRAWDOWNS
Strategy 1 vs. SPY
STRATEGY 1
SPY (S&P 500)
Strategy I avoided the major dips of the 2022 bear market and significantly reduced SPY's drawdowns
SPY
Strategy 1

8. How RISP 500 Protects Portfolios (More Proof!)

Seeing is believing. Let's shed some light on details of the protection objective of the RISP 500™ by showing how a 2-risk level strategy with the most basic strategy (SPY or Cash) would have performed during two major crashes: the 2020 Coronavirus Crash and the 2008 Global Financial Crisis. We are going to illustrate three levels of RPT: 70%, 80%, and 90%.

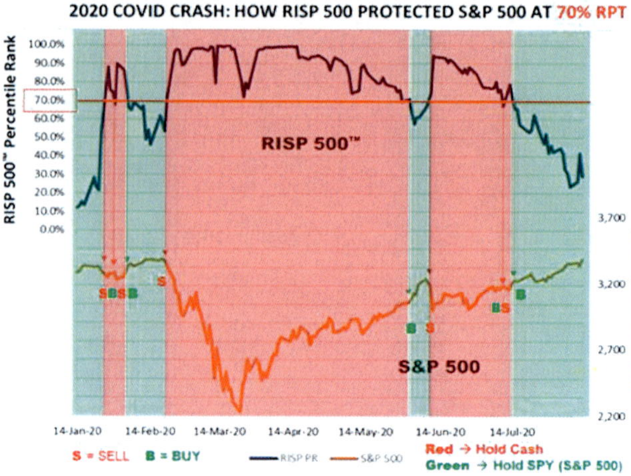
2020 COVID CRASH: HOW RISP 500 PROTECTED S&P 500 AT 70% RPT
RISP 500™ Percentile Rank
100.0%
90.0%
80.0%
70.0%
60.0%
50.0%
40.0%
30.0%
20.0%
10.0%
0.0%
RISP 500™
S&P 500
3,700
3,200
2,700
2,200
S&P 500 Index (points)
14-Jan-20
14-Feb-20
14-Mar-20
14-Apr-20
14-May-20
14-Jun-20
14-Jul-20
S = SELL
B = BUY
RISP PR
S&P 500
Red → Hold Cash
Green → Hold SPY (S&P 500)

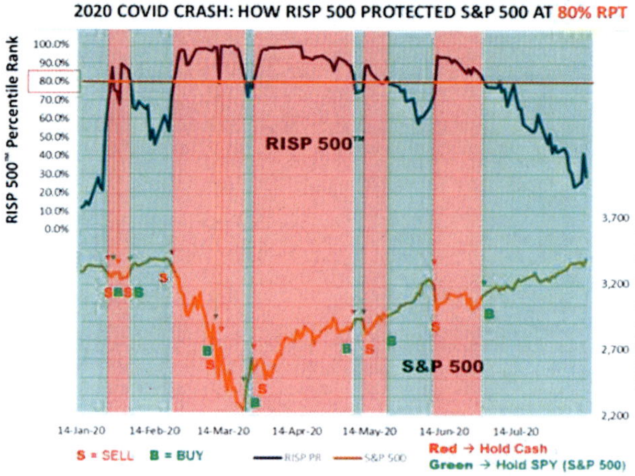
2020 COVID CRASH: HOW RISP 500 PROTECTED S&P 500 AT 80% RPT
RISP 500™ Percentile Rank
100.0%
90.0%
80.0%
70.0%
60.0%
50.0%
40.0%
30.0%
20.0%
10.0%
0.0%
RISP 500™
S&P 500
3,700
3,200
2,700
2,200
S&P 500 Index (points)
14-Jan-20
14-Feb-20
14-Mar-20
14-Apr-20
14-May-20
14-Jun-20
14-Jul-20
S = SELL
B = BUY
RISP PR
S&P 500
Red → Hold Cash
Green → Hold SPY (S&P 500)

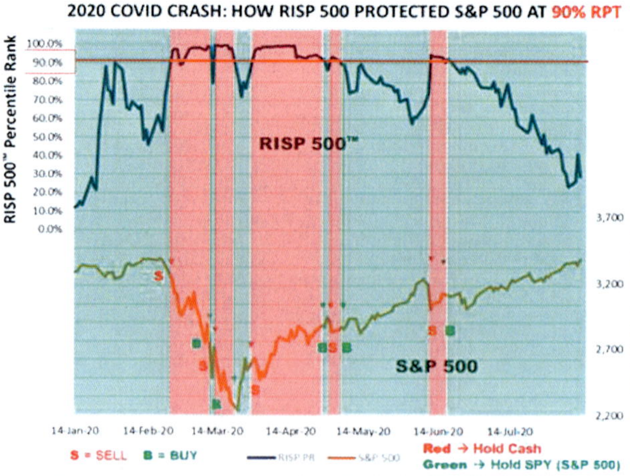
2020 COVID CRASH: HOW RISP 500 PROTECTED S&P 500 AT 90% RPT
RISP 500™ Percentile Rank
100.0%
90.0%
80.0%
70.0%
60.0%
50.0%
40.0%
30.0%
20.0%
10.0%
0.0%
RISP 500™
S&P 500
3,700
3,200
2,700
2,200
S&P 500 Index (points)
14-Jan-20
14-Feb-20
14-Mar-20
14-Apr-20
14-May-20
14-Jun-20
14-Jul-20
S = SELL
B = BUY
RISP PR
S&P 500
Red → Hold Cash
Green → Hold SPY (S&P 500)

2008 GFC: HOW RISP 500 PROTECTED S&P 500 AT 70% RPT

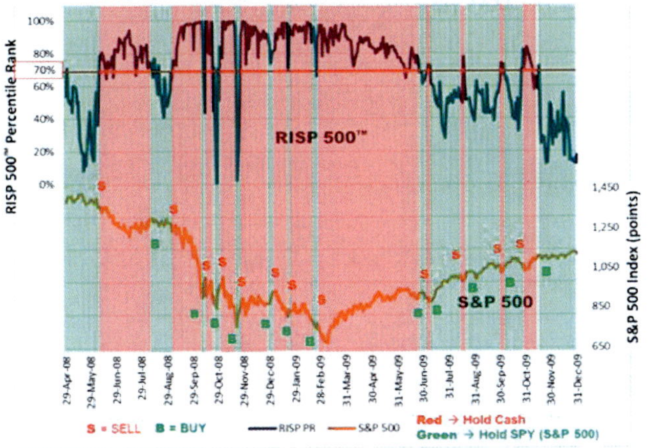

2008 GFC: HOW RISP 500 PROTECTED S&P 500 AT 80% RPT

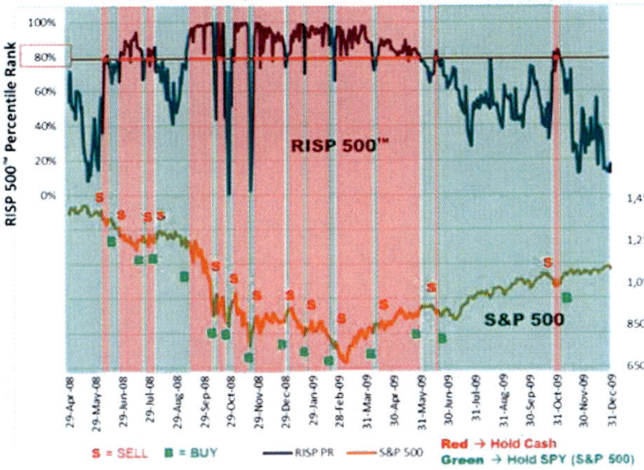

2008 GFC: HOW RISP 500 PROTECTED S&P 500 AT 90% RPT

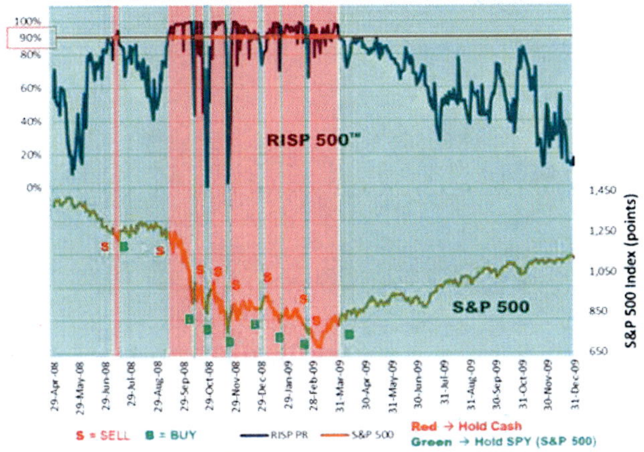

OTHER MAJOR CRASHES

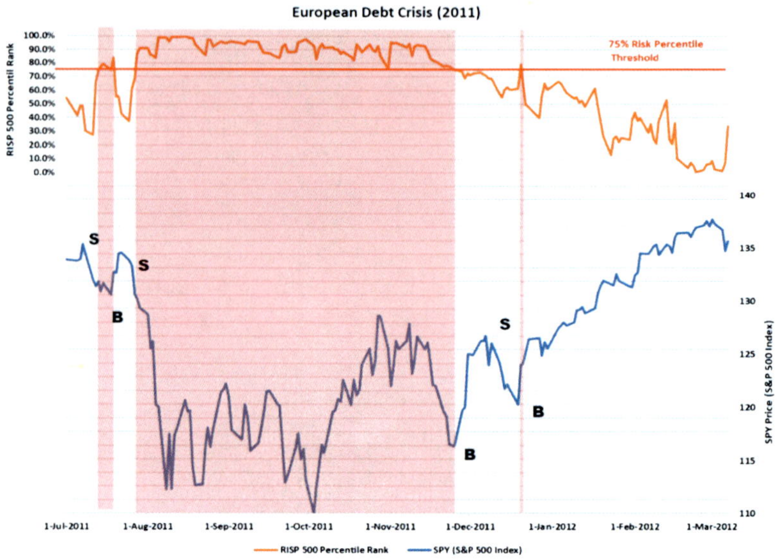

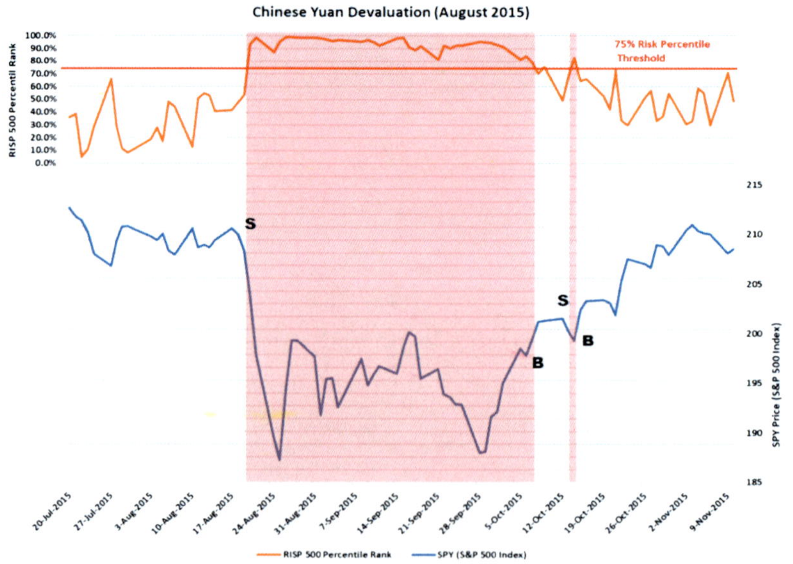

Brexit (June 2016)

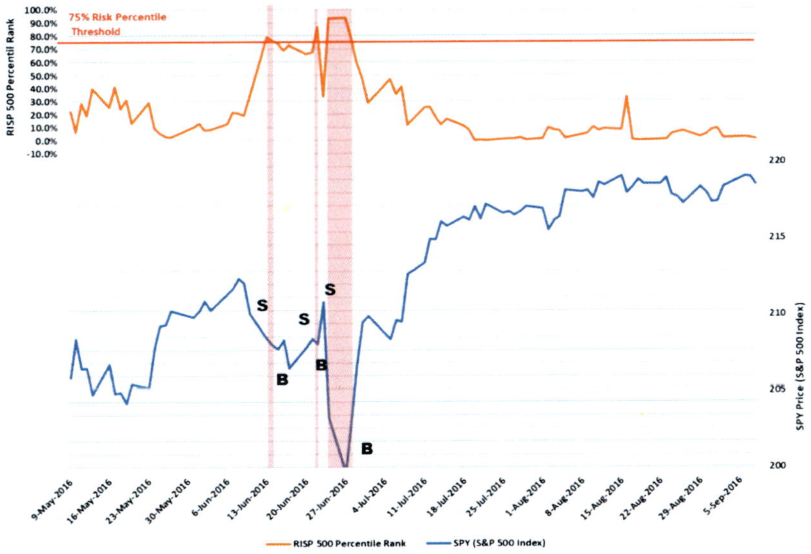

Volgameddon Crash (February 2018)

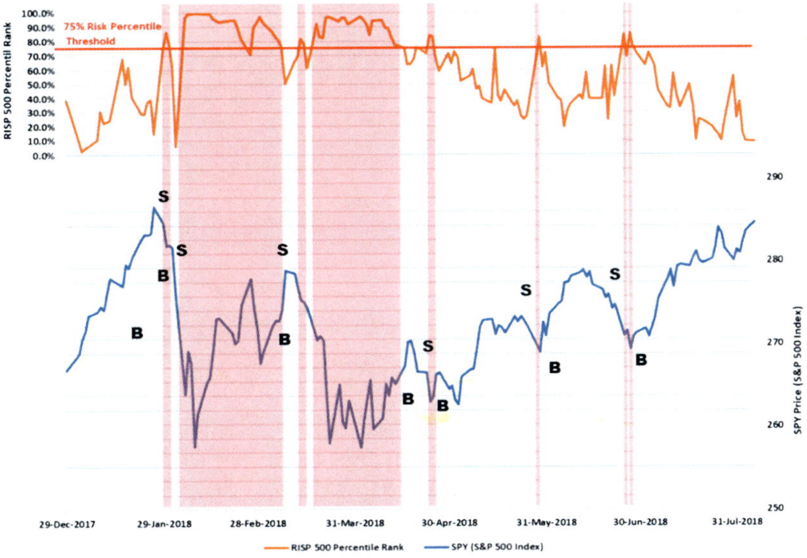

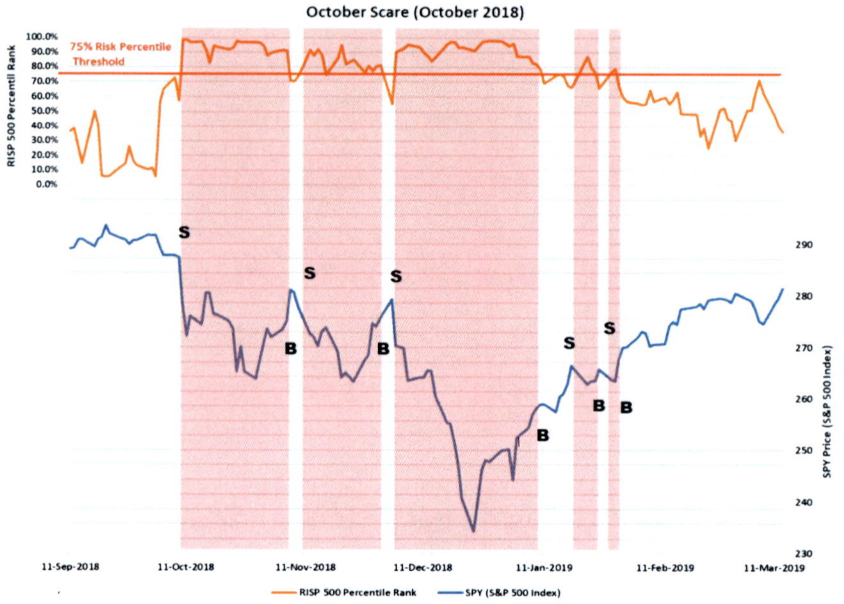
October Scare (October 2018)
RISP 500 Percentil Rank
100.0%
90.0%
80.0%
70.0%
60.0%
50.0%
40.0%
30.0%
20.0%
10.0%
0.0%
75% Risk Percentile
Threshold
S
S
S
B
B
S
S
B
B
B
290
280
270
260
250
240
230
SPY Price (S&P 500 Index)
11-Sep-2018
11-Oct-2018
11-Nov-2018
11-Dec-2018
11-Jan-2019
11-Feb-2019
11-Mar-2019
RISP 500 Percentile Rank
SPY (S&P 500 Index)

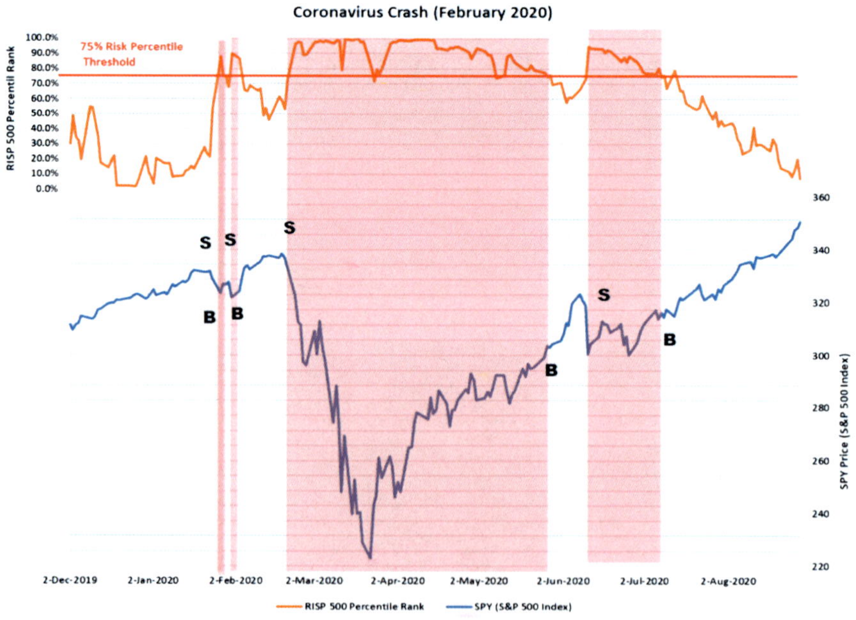
Coronavirus Crash (February 2020)
RISP 500 Percentil Rank
100.0%
90.0%
80.0%
70.0%
60.0%
50.0%
40.0%
30.0%
20.0%
10.0%
0.0%
75% Risk Percentile
Threshold
S
S
S
B
B
S
B
B
360
340
320
300
280
260
240
220
SPY Price (S&P 500 Index)
2-Dec-2019
2-Jan-2020
2-Feb-2020
2-Mar-2020
2-Apr-2020
2-May-2020
2-Jun-2020
2-Jul-2020
2-Aug-2020
RISP 500 Percentile Rank
SPY (S&P 500 Index)

RECENT MARKET ROUT (AUGUST 2024)

Last sold at **$552.90** (Aug 1, 2024)

Market closed at **$532.90** (Aug 2, 2024)

Last time bought at **$416.37** (Oct 31, 2023)

Date	RISP 500 value	Percentile Rank	RISK ON/OFF	Strategy 1 - ST-2L-SP500 (Based on S&P 500) Trade action	Trade price	SPY Close	Stop level	Stopped? YES/NO	Cycle #	Day's Return	YTD Return	LTD Return
11/9/2023	97.1	51.5%	On		-	433.84	424.13	No	27	-0.78%	17.78%	15.18%
11/8/2023	91.9	42.9%	On		-	437.25	423.82	No	27	0.07%	18.71%	16.09%
11/7/2023	93.8	45.8%	On		-	436.93	422.62	No	27	0.28%	18.62%	16.00%
11/6/2023	94.6	47.2%	On		-	435.69	421.65	No	27	0.23%	18.28%	15.68%
11/3/2023	91.3	41.4%	On		-	434.69	417.84	No	27	0.91%	18.01%	15.41%
11/2/2023	96.5	50.1%	On		-	430.76	409.98	No	27	1.92%	16.94%	14.37%
11/1/2023	104.1	62.8%	On		-	422.66	405.65	No	27	1.07%	14.74%	12.22%
10/31/2023	109.1	70.2%	On	Buy	416.37	418.2	403.88	No	27	0.44%	13.53%	11.03%
10/30/2023	114.7	77.4%	OFF		-	415.59	398.36		26	0.00%	13.04%	10.55%
10/27/2023	116.3	79.0%	OFF		-	410.68	400.17		26	0.00%	13.04%	10.55%

Date	RISP 500 value	Percentile Rank	RISK ON/OFF	Strategy 1 - ST-2L-SP500 (Based on S&P 500) Trade action	Trade price	SPY Close	Stop level	Stopped? YES/NO	Cycle #	Day's Return	YTD Return	LTD Return
8/2/2024	127.8	91.4%	OFF		-	532.9	534.29		31	0.00%	18.41%	58.48%
8/1/2024	115.2	77.8%	OFF	Sell	552.90	543.01	534.29		31	0.38%	18.41%	58.48%
7/31/2024	112.2	74.3%	On	Buy	548.41	550.81	531.96	No	31	0.44%	17.97%	57.88%
7/30/2024	113.4	75.7%	OFF		-	542	528.42		30	0.00%	17.45%	57.19%
7/29/2024	114.1	76.7%	OFF		-	544.76	528.11		30	0.00%	17.45%	57.19%
7/26/2024	115.6	78.0%	OFF		-	544.44	522.26		30	0.00%	17.45%	57.19%
7/25/2024	122.8	85.7%	OFF		-	538.41	538.01		30	0.00%	17.45%	57.19%
7/24/2024	114.9	77.5%	OFF	Sell	548.21	541.23	538.01		30	-1.01%	17.45%	57.19%
7/23/2024	103.1	61.6%	On		-	553.78	538.01	No	30	-0.16%	18.65%	58.79%
7/22/2024	109.2	70.2%	On	Buy	551.47	554.65	534.93	No	30	0.58%	18.83%	59.04%
7/19/2024	115.8	78.3%	OFF	Sell	553.43	548.99	547.91		29	0.14%	18.15%	58.13%
7/18/2024	96.7	50.4%	On		-	552.66	547.91	No	29	-0.77%	17.99%	57.91%
7/17/2024	93.3	44.9%	On		-	556.94	547.91	No	29	-1.40%	18.90%	59.13%
7/16/2024	90.7	40.2%	On		-	564.86	544.68	No	29	0.59%	20.59%	61.39%
7/15/2024	90.7	40.4%	On		-	561.53	543.19	No	29	0.28%	19.88%	60.44%
7/12/2024	81.5	23.6%	On		-	559.99	544.48	No	29	0.63%	19.55%	60.00%
7/11/2024	93.1	44.6%	On		-	556.48	544.48	No	29	-0.86%	18.80%	59.00%
7/10/2024	84.7	29.3%	On		-	561.32	539.15	No	29	0.99%	19.84%	60.38%
7/9/2024	85.4	30.7%	On		-	555.82	538.62	No	29	0.10%	18.66%	58.81%
7/8/2024	87.9	35.1%	On		-	555.28	538.00	No	29	0.12%	18.55%	58.65%

FINAL CHAPTER

A New Era in Wealth Management Awaits

As you close this book, you're starting a journey with a truly dynamic, data-driven approach that transforms risk into opportunity. You now hold the blueprint to outperform benchmarks, protect wealth during turbulent times, and redefine the very limits of what's achievable for your clients. The SMIGRM method, anchored by the RISP 500™ indicator, brings a decisive advantage to the table—an advantage that's now within your reach.

A CATALYST TO DELIVER RESULTS AND GROW AUM

Imagine advising your clients with the confidence that **whatever the market's direction is, your strategy is always aligned and optimized to deal with any market condition (bull, bear, stagnant, or volatile).** The Context-Dependent Dynamic Asset Allocation pillar of SMIGRM means you can quickly adapt to ever changing market conditions and sentiment, moving between asset classes according to actual measurable risk levels.

Imagine the power of the RISP 500™ **combined with your own skills as an investment manager**. This combination has the potential to take your business to the next level and differentiate you from your peer competitors in the wealth management industry.

With the direction the global economy is heading, in conjunction of an emerging new world order, greater nation competition, resurging inflationary pressures, geopolitical conflicts, the effects of global warming, societal polarization, higher volatility, and so many other sources of uncertainty for the next 10, 20 years and beyond, plus the disruptions caused by AI and investor behavioral shifts (e.g., passive investing, etc.), successful wealth managers need to always stay one step ahead. SMIGRM was developed because of our vision that the world post-2008 will be a radically different one that is a lot more challenging for the entire wealth management industry.

You might be thinking, "I've seen other systems and methodologies come and go. How is this different?" Unlike most systems, SMIGRM isn't a closed formula. We aren't instant internet sensationalists appearing as overnight YouTube "experts" offering magic bullets to make millionaires in the stock market. These folks prey on the unwary individual investor but are scared to offer their solutions to industry professionals like we do. We offer solutions to wealth managers because we are confident that we have a solid product. We are a serious risk management research lab run by professionals with real industry experience (especially from multiple financial crises over 3 decades) constantly testing the data and recalibrating variables and parameters of the algorithm as necessary to keep it sharp and up-to-date. The model needs to adapt to new market regimes and unprecedented events, drawing on data inputs that keep it responsive, relevant, and ahead of market shifts. This flexibility is the critical difference. And we provided not only past data to prove how the RISP 500™ protected wealth during major crashes but also how it is still protecting wealth, day after day, by making public our daily performance.

As a financial professional, your success rests on the value you bring to your clients. With the RISP 500™, you're not just managing wealth—you're setting new standards in proactive risk management, capitalizing on the latest advancements in the state-of-the-art science applied to financial markets and risk management.

Moreover, SMIGRM's approach isn't about replacing your expertise but enhancing it with cutting-edge tools that can amplify your ability to deliver consistent, superior results to your most demanding wealthy clients.

JOIN THE MOVEMENT TO REDEFINE WEALTH MANAGEMENT

The best way to understand the power of SMIGRM is to experience it firsthand. Why not give it a try with a small portion of your portfolio just to test it out? You can easily test it with an ETF for less than $1,000 or simply compare with your own results to see if using RISP 500™ would have led you to stronger results. To make it a really no-brainer decision for even the most skeptical wealth manager, **we decided to make RISP 500™ available in Beta for FREE so that wealth managers can test drive it themselves live**.

But don't delay because it's for a **limited time only**. Sign up for a **no-risk, free trial of the RISP 500™ indicator at www.engineering-finance.com**. You have nothing to lose because it's **FREE** and you can try with very little money if you're still skeptical. What if all you have learned in this book turns out to be a game changer for you, your money, and your clients' money? We are totally confident that the return-to-risk ratio here is more than favorable for you. Whether you're managing millions in client assets or just testing with a small portion of your portfolio, the RISP 500™ can help you achieve real results.

- Protect wealth during volatile markets and crashes through early detection.
- Enhance returns by only taking risks worth taking.
- Amplify returns by safely exploring risk during market rallies.

- Create your own strategies or fit RISP 500™ to your existing portfolio strategies.
- Achieve wealth preservation with high returns and keep your clients happy wanting more.
- Differentiate yourself in the competitive wealth management industry.

Your journey to outperform yourself and redefine wealth management starts now.

We Provide 100% Customized Services to Funds and Wealth Management Firms

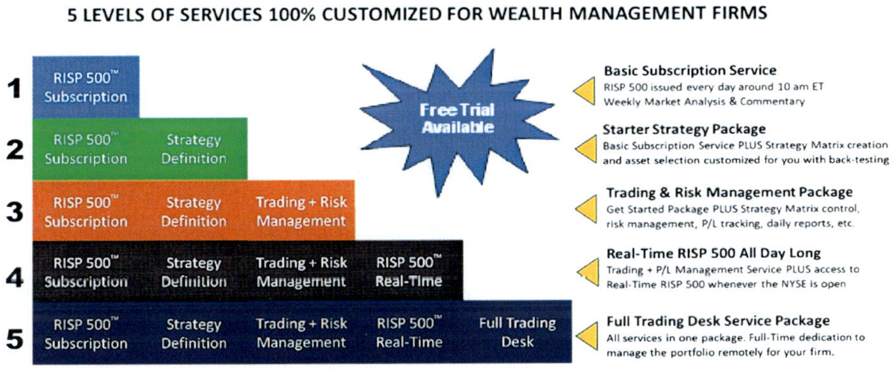

Are you ready to take your investment management business to the next level with the RISP 500™?

We are here to help you all the way to outperformance. Your clients deserve only the very best, never forget that. You want the best tools you can possibly land your hands on to deliver the best investing performance results possible. As our client, you deserve the best too, so we strive to deliver the best service possible to you.

We designed 5 levels of services 100% customizable to meet your unique needs. Send us a message so that we start answering your questions and establish a relationship. We offer a free trial period so you have the opportunity to experience what it is like to receive the RISP 500™ measured every day in your mailbox. This is information you can start acting upon and make money even during the trial period.

E-Mail: VIPclientservice@risp500.com
www.Engineering-Finance.com

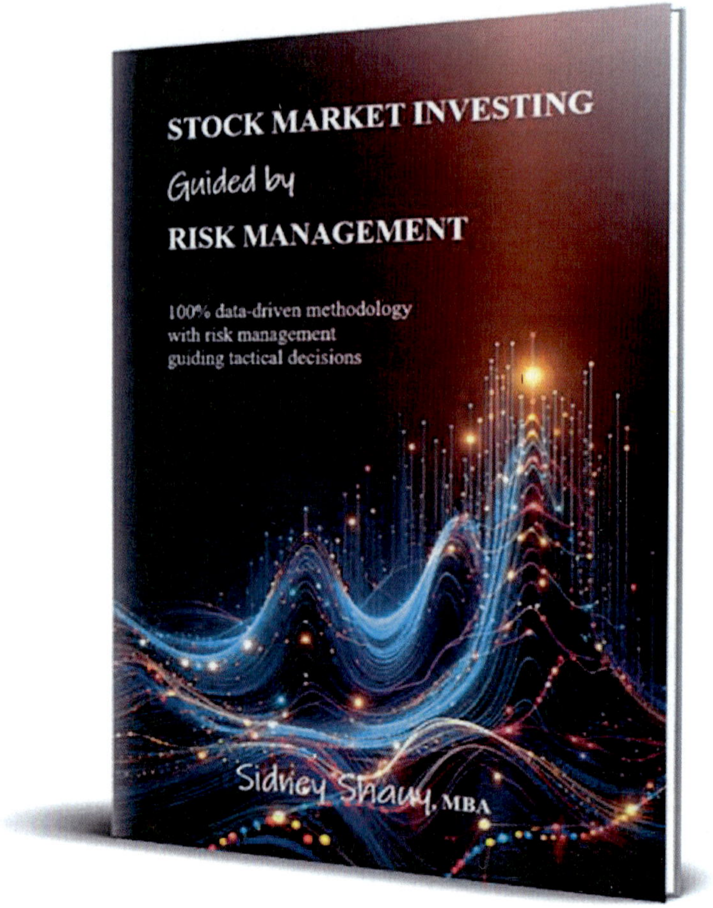

We wrote a book titled "**Stock Market Investing Guided by Risk Management**" published on Amazon, to explain the entire concept of SMIGRM in much greater detail, including the science behind the RISP 500 algorithm.

https://www.amazon.com/Stock-Market-Investing-Guided-Management/dp/1960691104

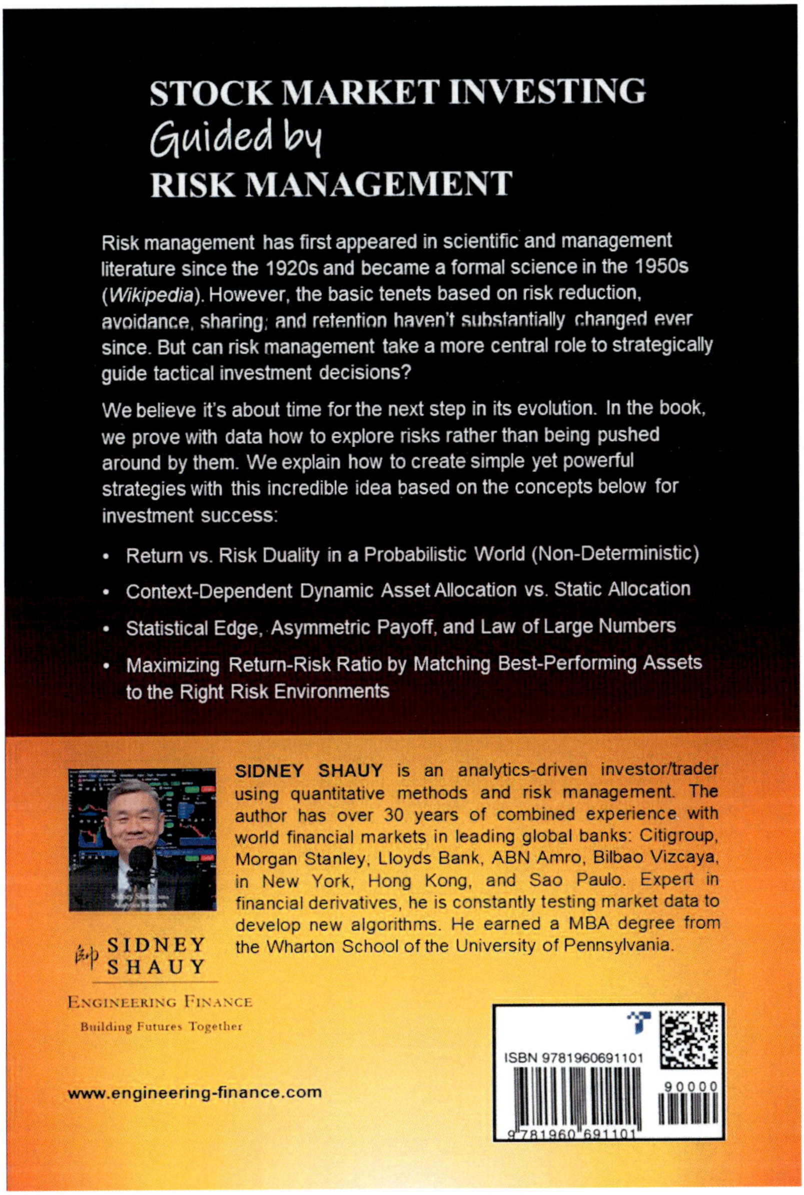
STOCK MARKET INVESTING
Guided by
RISK MANAGEMENT
Risk management has first appeared in scientific and management literature since the 1920s and became a formal science in the 1950s (Wikipedia). However, the basic tenets based on risk reduction, avoidance, sharing, and retention haven't substantially changed ever since. But can risk management take a more central role to strategically guide tactical investment decisions?
We believe it's about time for the next step in its evolution. In the book, we prove with data how to explore risks rather than being pushed around by them. We explain how to create simple yet powerful strategies with this incredible idea based on the concepts below for investment success:
• Return vs. Risk Duality in a Probabilistic World (Non-Deterministic)
• Context-Dependent Dynamic Asset Allocation vs. Static Allocation
• Statistical Edge, Asymmetric Payoff, and Law of Large Numbers
• Maximizing Return-Risk Ratio by Matching Best-Performing Assets to the Right Risk Environments
SIDNEY SHAUY is an analytics-driven investor/trader using quantitative methods and risk management. The author has over 30 years of combined experience with world financial markets in leading global banks: Citigroup, Morgan Stanley, Lloyds Bank, ABN Amro, Bilbao Vizcaya, in New York, Hong Kong, and Sao Paulo. Expert in financial derivatives, he is constantly testing market data to develop new algorithms. He earned a MBA degree from the Wharton School of the University of Pennsylvania.
SIDNEY SHAUY
ENGINEERING FINANCE
Building Futures Together
www.engineering-finance.com
ISBN 9781960691101
90000
9 781960 691101

Performance Acceleration Mentorship Coaching Programs (For Individual Investors)

We understand that everyone has a different learning style, has a unique blend of needs and goals, and may be at a different point on the learning curve. Mentorship is focused on implementation and it's goals-based. For more information, be sure to sign up for our free newsletter to be informed of new programs and other educational resources on our website: www.engineering-finance.com.

Customized Services to Financial Advisors, Professional Investors, Wealth Management Firms and Fund Managers

Risk Scientific LLC offers special services to financial advisors, professional investors, wealth management firms, and fund managers. Contact us by email: VIPclientservice@risp500.com.

Final Words of Gratitude

I hope I was able to meet your expectations when you set out to read this book. Writing the book took me great effort, so I hope I was able to deliver real value to you. I also hope you will be able to make good use of what you learned here to transform your life, if you are an investor, or the life of your clients, if you are a wealth manager.

I would like to offer my words of gratitude for your trust. After "speaking" so much, now I wish to hear what you have to say. I only ask you to leave me your honest assessment as feedback to help me improve myself as an author and communicator. I truly value what you think! I would very much appreciate an honest review on Amazon:

https://www.Amazon.com/review/create-review?&asin=B0DP856WBM

Your input will guide my next steps to create better content, make changes, improve, and better help everyone.

Thank you! 😊

Sidney Shauy, MBA

www.Engineering-Finance.com

Made in United States
North Haven, CT
06 November 2026

21791730R00051